The Mane Attraction

The Mane Attraction

Exploring Lion Cranial Anatomy

Sanyub S

UNIEK ENTERPRISES

CONTENTS

INDEX

Introduction

1. A brief overview of the significance of studying lion cranial anatomy.
2. The role of the mane and its relation to cranial features.
3. Importance in understanding the evolutionary adaptations of big cats.

Chapter 1 Evolutionary History
1.1 Tracing the evolutionary journey of lions and their ancestors.
1.2 Comparative analysis with other big cat species.
1.3 Exploration of fossil evidence revealing cranial adaptations.

Chapter 2 External Cranial Features
2.1 Detailed examination of the lion's external skull structure.
2.2 Significance of the mane in male lions and its cranial implications.
2..3 Adaptations for powerful biting and securing prey.

Chapter 3 Internal Cranial Structures
3.1 In-depth analysis of the lion's internal cranial anatomy.
3.2 Exploration of the brain size, structure, and its correlation with behavior.
3.3 Examination of sensory adaptations, including vision and olfaction.

Chapter 4 Functionality of the Jaw and Teeth
4.1 Understanding the powerful bite force of lions.
4.2 Analysis of dental adaptations for hunting and feeding.
4.3 Implications for survival and ecological niche.

Chapter 5 Communication through Cranial Features
5.1 Investigating the role of cranial anatomy in lion communication.
5.2 Vocalization mechanisms and their connection to cranial structures.
5.3 Social implications of communication within prides.

Chapter 6 Pathologies and Anomalies

6.1Exploration of common cranial pathologies in captive and wild lions.

6.2Impact of environmental factors on cranial health.

6.3The role of research in mitigating cranial anomalies in conservation.

Chapter 7 Technological Advances in Cranial Studies

7.1Overview of modern techniques in studying lion cranial anatomy.

7.2Radiographic and imaging methods for detailed analysis.

7.3Contributions to broader fields, including paleontology and veterinary science.

Chapter 8 Conservation Implications

8.1Discussing how understanding cranial anatomy aids in conservation efforts.

8.2The role of genetic diversity in maintaining healthy cranial features.

8.3Challenges and opportunities in preserving lion populations.

Chapter 9 Future Directions in Cranial Anatomy Research

9.1Emerging areas of study and research opportunities.

9.2Integrating technology and traditional methods for comprehensive insights.

9.3The potential impact of cranial research on broader scientific fields.

The lion, adored as the "ruler of the wilderness," has long caught the creative mind of humankind with its grand presence and unmatched moxy. While its whole body adds to its striking picture, a specific feature stands apart as the exemplification of glory — the notable mane. In this extensive investigation, we leave on an excursion profound into the core of the lion's cranial life systems, disentangling the organic complexities that characterize its head, from the strong skull to the emblematic and practical meaning of the great mane.

The Physical Wonder of the Lion's Skull

At the groundwork of understanding the lion's cranial life structures lies the multifaceted design of its skull. Development has shaped a noteworthy harmony among strength and spryness, furnishing the lion with an amazing asset for endurance. The skull's strong design houses considerable jaw muscles, a demonstration of the savage idea of these dominant hunters. The huge, pointed canines and sharp molars highlight the effectiveness with which lions tear through tissue and crunch bones, exhibiting their ability as gifted trackers in the animals of the world collectively.

The Imagery of the Mane: A Crown of Solidarity and Development

While the lion's skull establishes the groundwork for its actual ability, the colorful and unmistakable mane hoists the animal to a notable status. Made out of thick, long hair surrounding the head and neck, the mane isn't simply a stylish frivolity yet an image of solidarity and development. As we investigate the developmental ramifications of this particular element, a more profound comprehension of its job in friendly elements and individual character inside the pride becomes visible.

Variations for Social Elements

The mane's importance stretches out past simple feel; it assumes a significant part in the perplexing social elements of lion prides. A more full and hazier mane frequently corresponds with a lion's raised status inside the gathering, mirroring its development and ability. This obvious sign turns into its very own language, passing on data about a singular lion's wellbeing and imperativeness. It fills in as an honorable symbol, a demonstration of the difficulties survive and the strength showed in the cruel African savannah.

Mane as a Safeguard: Usefulness in Nature

The lion's mane isn't just an image; it serves down to earth capabilities in the difficult conditions where these animals wander. During regional questions or conflicts with rival guys, the mane changes into a defensive safeguard.

Its thickness gives an actual hindrance, deflecting foes by making an impressive outline and causing the lion to seem bigger and more considerable. This double job of the mane, as both an image and a useful resource, mirrors the unpredictable embroidery of transformations woven by development.

Visual Correspondence and Individual Character

In the immense breadths of the African wild, where prides explore complex social designs, the mane turns into a device of visual correspondence. Lions, naturally, are exceptionally friendly creatures, and the particular appearance of every mane adds to the visual character inside the pride. As we dive into the correspondence parts of the mane, we disentangle the quiet language spoken through prepping customs, stances, and the unpredictable elements of pride life.

The Transformative Importance

To really see the value in the mane's appeal, following its developmental trajectory is fundamental. Understanding how this striking element formed offers bits of knowledge into the versatile benefits it presented upon the species. Transformative scholars and scientistss give important points of view on the improvement of the mane, revealing insight into its part in sexual determination, security, and as an obvious signal for the two opponents and expected mates.

Protection Suggestions

Past the domains of science and transformative history, the investigation of lion cranial life structures holds importance for contemporary preservation endeavors. As the lion faces dangers going from territory misfortune to human-natural life struggle, an extensive comprehension of its life structures turns into a foundation for informed protection systems. We investigate the crossing point of science and protection, digging into how the safeguarding of this famous species includes safeguarding their natural surroundings as well as grasping the perplexing subtleties of their physiology.

The Excursion Ahead

This complete investigation of the mane as a point of convergence in lion cranial life structures is an excursion into the core of perhaps of nature's most famous animal. From the organic wonders of the skull to the representative and useful meaning of the mane, every aspect adds to the glorious atmosphere that encompasses the ruler of monsters. As we unwind the intricacies, we gain a significant appreciation for the fragile equilibrium of nature that has shaped this superb species over centuries. Go along with us on this odyssey into the core of the lion, where science, imagery, and the wild unite in an orchestra of nature's loftiness.

1. **A brief overview of the significance of studying lion cranial anatomy.**
The lion, Panthera leo, orders consideration as quite possibly of the most notable and appealling specie in the set of all animals. Past its glorious mane and majestic disposition, the investigation of lion cranial life structures opens a store of experiences into the transformative, natural, and conduct parts of this grand animal. This article gives a thorough outline of the meaning of digging into the complexities of lion cranial life structures, revealing insight into the more extensive ramifications for preservation, transformative science, and our comprehension of the perplexing elements inside lion prides.

Developmental Bits of knowledge:

Versatile Advancement:

The assessment of lion cranial life structures fills in as an entryway to figuring out the versatile development of this species. Developmental scholars investigate cranial elements to perceive how lions have adjusted to their environmental specialty, disentangling the specific tensions that have formed their skull structure north of millions of years.

Paleontological Importance:

Fossils and near investigations of surviving lions and their terminated family members give a worldly viewpoint on the development of lion cranial life structures. Scientistss examine these old remaining parts to follow changes in skull morphology, contributing important information to the more extensive field of vertebrate fossil science.

Practical Morphology:

Savage Variations:

The cranial life systems of lions, especially the design of the skull and jaw, is unpredictably connected to their job as dominant hunters. Concentrating on these variations uncovers the biomechanics behind their strong chomps and concentrated dentition, giving bits of knowledge into their hunting systems and the environmental connections inside their environments.

Taking care of Conduct:

Lion cranial life systems is a vital consider grasping their taking care of conduct. Inspecting highlights, for example, tooth morphology and jaw mechanics empowers analysts to perceive the dietary inclinations of lions, going from the tearing of tissue to the pulverizing of bones. This information adds to how we might interpret hunter prey collaborations and environment elements.

Social Elements and Correspondence:

Mane as a Social Sign:

The investigation of lion cranial life systems stretches out to the representative meaning of the mane. Specialists dive into the connection between mane attributes and social elements inside prides, disentangling how varieties in mane size and variety might pass on data about a singular lion's age, wellbeing, and social standing.

Visual Correspondence:

Lions are exceptionally friendly creatures, and their correspondence goes past vocalizations. The peculiarity of cranial elements, including the mane, adds to visual correspondence inside the pride. Preparing ceremonies, stances, and the general appearance of a singular's skull and mane assume a part in passing on data inside the gathering.

Protection Suggestions:

Populace Wellbeing Evaluation:

The investigation of lion cranial life systems gives a harmless technique to evaluating the wellbeing and hereditary variety of populaces. Morphological varieties can offer experiences into the general prosperity of lion populaces, helping progressives in observing and dealing with these magnetic species.

Human-Natural life Struggle Alleviation:

Understanding lion cranial life structures is critical in moderating human-natural life struggle. By understanding the elements affecting lion conduct, progressives can foster systems to decrease clashes, guaranteeing the conjunction of lions and nearby networks.

Safeguarding of Cornerstone Species:

Lions assume a vital part as cornerstone species, impacting the construction and capability of environments. Concentrating on their cranial life systems supports perceiving the environmental meaning of lions and highlights the requirement for their protection to keep up with adjusted and sound environments.

Innovative Headways:

Advancements in Imaging Innovation:

Innovative headways, like figured tomography (CT) sweeps and three-layered imaging, have altered the investigation of cranial life systems. These devices consider nitty gritty assessments of interior designs, giving scientists exceptional bits of knowledge into the complexities of lion skulls without the requirement for obtrusive techniques.

Genomic Approaches:

The joining of genomic approaches with cranial life structures concentrates on upgrades how we might interpret the hereditary reason for cranial variety. Scientists can investigate the qualities answerable for skull advancement, revealing insight into the sub-atomic components that add to the different cranial morphologies saw in lion populaces.

Instructive and Effort Open doors:

Public Commitment:

The investigation of lion cranial life structures presents novel instructive open doors for people in general. Connecting with stories about the meaning of cranial highlights, like the mane, dazzle crowds, cultivating a more profound appreciation for natural life and the significance of protection.

Logical Effort:

Joint effort among specialists and teachers works with the interpretation of intricate logical discoveries into open data. This effort encourages a more extensive comprehension of the meaning of lion cranial life structures, interfacing mainstream researchers with people in general and earning support for preservation drives.

Future Headings:

Proceeded with Exploration:

As innovation develops, the investigation of lion cranial life structures is ready for proceeded with headways. Future exploration might include greater genomic investigations, refined imaging methods, and interdisciplinary coordinated efforts that develop how we might interpret these dominant hunters.

Protection Procedures:

The bits of knowledge gathered from concentrating on lion cranial life structures will assume a vital part in forming designated protection systems. Versatile administration, informed by continuous examination, will direct endeavors to safeguard the actual lions as well as the environments they occupy.

2. **The role of the mane and its relation to cranial features.**

The lion, Panthera leo, flaunts an evident mystique, and quite a bit of its charm lies in the dazzling presence of the famous mane. Past its stylish allure, the lion's mane holds a mind boggling relationship with its cranial elements, unwinding a story that traverses developmental importance, useful transformations, and unpredictable social elements inside prides.

Developmental Starting points and Importance:

The development of the lion's mane is unpredictably associated with sexual choice, featuring its job as an obvious sign for hereditary wellness and in general wellbeing. Research proposes that the mane fills in as an unmistakable consider mate fascination, with females showing an inclination for guys with more full and hazier manes. This association between the mane and conceptive achievement highlights its transformative importance as an image of imperativeness and allure inside the species.

Cranial Highlights and Mane Changeability:

The changeability in lion mane qualities is intently attached to the lion's cranial highlights. Lions with bigger, more vigorous skulls frequently display more full and additional overwhelming manes. This connection proposes a unique exchange between hereditary elements, in general wellbeing, and the size of cranial designs. The investigation of cranial highlights subsequently turns into a passage to figuring out the variety in mane appearances among individual lions.

Social Elements and Mane Varieties:

Inside the complex social ordered progression of lion prides, the mane assumes a significant part in showing predominance and social standing. Lions with more full and hazier manes are frequently connected with raised status, adding to their capacity to attest strength during social associations inside the pride. Mane varieties become essential to the visual correspondence inside the pride, working with speedy acknowledgment and cultivating effective participation during bunch exercises.

Useful Transformations and Mane as a Defensive Safeguard:

The useful parts of the lion's cranial life systems, especially the jaw and teeth transformations, are intently attached to the turn of events and upkeep of the mane. The strong jaw muscles and strong dentition are fundamental for the lion's ruthless way of life as well as add to the defensive capability of the mane. During conflicts and regional questions, the voluminous appearance of the mane makes a monumental outline, going about as a visual obstacle and improving the lion's opportunities to effectively guard its domain.

Past the visual angle, the thick fur of the mane gives actual insurance during battle. Going about as a pad, it safeguards the lion's neck and throat from nibbles and scratches during forceful experiences with rivals or while hunting huge prey. This double job of the mane, as both a visual and actual obstacle, features its versatile importance in improving the lion's survivability.

Preparing and Social Holding:

mane turns into an essential part of prepping ceremonies inside lion prides. Common preparing is a social holding action that builds up friendly union and pecking order. Mane-pulling and licking during prepping ceremonies add to the upkeep of positive social elements inside the pride. Moreover, the job of the mane stretches out to maternal cooperations, where lionesses participate in preparing exercises including the male's mane, encouraging positive social bonds that add to the general prosperity of the pride.

Mane Improvement and Ecological Impacts:

The turn of events and presence of the mane are affected by hereditary elements as well as by ecological circumstances. The accessibility of food assets and by and large natural circumstances can influence the size and thickness of the mane. Lions in very much supported conditions might display more vigorous manes, while those in less good circumstances might have more modest manes. Furthermore, environment assumes a part, with lions in more blazing districts possibly having more modest manes as an intensity directing transformation. This natural adaptability features the mane's job in answering different biological difficulties.

Protection Suggestions:

Concentrating on the connection between the mane and cranial highlights holds critical ramifications for lion preservation. Checking varieties in mane qualities can give important experiences into the wellbeing and hereditary variety of lion populaces. Progressives can utilize this data to survey and oversee populaces really, adding to the conservation of this charming species.

Understanding the job of the mane in friendly flagging and regional protection illuminates preservation procedures pointed toward moderating human-untamed life struggle. Protectionists can foster methodologies that limit possible struggles by thinking about the impact of mane attributes on lion conduct. The investigation of lion cranial elements, related to mane varieties, turns into a fundamental device in the preservationist's tool stash for guaranteeing the conjunction of lions and human networks.

3. **Importance in understanding the evolutionary adaptations of big cat**

The large felines, a lofty and considerable gathering of hunters, have spellbound the human creative mind for quite a long time. From the covert panther to the strong lion, these animals inspire a feeling of stunningness and esteem. To really see the value in the pith of huge felines, one should dig into the complex embroidery of their transformative variations.

Understanding the transformative excursion of huge felines isn't simply a scholastic pursuit; it uncovers significant bits of knowledge into their methods for surviving, environmental jobs, and the fragile equilibrium of our planet's biological systems.

The Developmental Timetable:

The narrative of large feline development traverses a long period of time, a demonstration of the consistently changing scene of our planet. The foundations of their lineage can be followed back to the family Felidae, which arose around quite a while back. The transformative timetable uncovers a progression of variations that have permitted enormous felines to flourish in different conditions, from thick wildernesses to far reaching savannahs.

One of the essential minutes in huge feline development happened around a long time back with the dissimilarity of Panthera, the variety that incorporates lions, tigers, panthers, and pumas, from different felids. This split denoted the start of the novel qualities that characterize enormous felines today.

Variations for Hunting:

The sign of huge felines lies in their excellent hunting ability. The advancement of specific highlights for hunting mirrors the constant tensions of regular choice. Think about the retractable hooks and strong appendages of the cheetah, empowering unparalleled speed and spryness. Such variations have permitted huge felines to become dominant hunters, finely tuned to seek after, catch, and stifle prey.

The advancement of binocular vision is another essential transformation. Hunters with front oriented eyes, similar to those of enormous felines, have profundity insight, permitting them to precisely pass judgment on distances. This transformation is significant during pursuits and ambushes, giving a competitive edge in the perplexing dance among hunter and prey.

Morphological Specializations:

The morphological transformations of enormous felines are a demonstration of the variety of their living spaces. The cover examples of the panther's jacket, for instance, are finely tuned to the dappled daylight of the wilderness, offering an ideal mix into the shadows. Interestingly, the sandy tone of a lion's mane matches the brilliant grasses of the African savannah, giving camouflage during the pivotal minutes before a snare.

The development of vigorous jaws and sharp teeth is a reaction to the requirement for productive carnivory. Large felines depend on their impressive dentition for catching prey as well as for consuming it. This specialization addresses the perplexing connection among structure and capability in the transformative cycle.

Social Designs and Helpful Hunting:

Past individual variations, the advancement of large felines has likewise led to complex social designs. Lions, for example, show a one of a kind social association with prides drove by prevailing guys. This collective living course of action gives benefits like agreeable hunting, insurance of youthful whelps, and regional guard.

Helpful hunting is a striking illustration of how social designs improve the effectiveness of enormous felines as hunters. Lions, cooperating in composed endeavors, can bring down prey that would be outside the realm of possibilities for single trackers to repress. This conduct exhibits the versatile meaning of sociality in the transformative progress of specific huge feline species.

Ecological Effects on Advancement:

The conditions where enormous felines developed play had a vital impact in forming their variations. The many-sided transaction among hunters and their environments features the fragile equilibrium that exists in nature. For instance, the thick vegetation of tropical rainforests has impacted the development of lithe climbers like the panther, giving them the capacity to explore the complicated overhang in quest for prey.

In open fields, the development of speed in cheetahs is a reaction to the broad scenes and the requirement for quick pursuits. These models highlight the close association between the actual climate and the developmental transformations of enormous felines, building up the idea of environmental specialties.

Environmental Change and Variation:

The continuous changes in worldwide environment designs have significant ramifications for the developmental direction of huge felines. These animals, finely receptive to their particular territories, face uncommon difficulties as their surroundings go through change. Changes in temperature, precipitation, and vegetation can modify prey overflow, water sources, and the general elements of environments, requiring versatile reactions from large felines.

Understanding how enormous felines adapt to and adjust to environmental change is vital for preservation endeavors. Preservationists and scientists should screen these transformations near carry out viable techniques that guarantee the endurance of these superb hunters even with a quickly influencing world.

Protection Suggestions:

The significance of understanding the transformative variations of enormous felines stretches out past logical interest; it has direct ramifications for protection endeavors. Human exercises, like environment obliteration, poaching, and environmental change, present huge dangers to the endurance of enormous feline species around the world.

A complete comprehension of their developmental history furnishes protectionists with significant experiences into the particular necessities and weaknesses of every species.

For example, the information that specific huge felines have adjusted to explicit prey or environments illuminates preservation methodologies pointed toward safeguarding these vital components. The distinguishing proof of key developmental characteristics can direct the making of safeguarded regions, passageways for movement, and drives that relieve the effect of human exercises on huge feline populaces.

Clinical Experiences from Large Feline Genomics:

As of late, headways in genomic research have opened new roads for figuring out the developmental transformations of huge felines. The sequencing of large feline genomes gives significant data about their hereditary variety, transformative connections, and likely variations to evolving conditions. Besides, concentrating on enormous feline genomics can offer bits of knowledge into the hereditary premise of infections, weakness to microbes, and potential protection systems.

The correlation of enormous feline genomes with their homegrown partners, like homegrown felines, can uncover the hereditary underpinnings of explicit variations and ways of behaving. This interdisciplinary methodology, consolidating genomics with conventional environmental investigations, holds guarantee for a more all encompassing comprehension of huge feline development.

Instructive Importance:

The transformative story of huge felines isn't just a logical undertaking yet in addition an instructive account that can move wonder and appreciation for the normal world. Finding out about the variations of huge felines cultivates a feeling of association with the more extensive trap of life and supports ecological stewardship. Instructive projects that underscore the transformative excursion of enormous felines can assume a urgent part in encouraging a more profound comprehension of biodiversity, environmental elements, and the significance of protection.

Zoos and natural life safe-havens, by exhibiting the different transformations of huge felines, add to public mindfulness and backing for preservation drives. Besides, instructive effort programs that feature the transformative wonders of these hunters can ignite interest and a feeling of obligation for the prosperity of these species and their natural surroundings.

Chapter 1

Evolutionary History

The tale of life on Earth is a striking account that traverses billions of years, enveloping the ascent and fall of incalculable species and the constant transformation to always evolving conditions. Transformative history is the fantastic woven artwork that winds around together the strings of hereditary variety, normal choice, and ecological tensions. From the modest starting points of single-celled organic entities to the mind boggling trap of life we see today, the excursion of development is a demonstration of the strength and imagination of nature.

The Beginning of Life:

The beginnings of life stay quite possibly of the most charming and discussed subject in established researchers. While the specific components that prompted the development of life are not completely perceived, researchers have proposed different speculations. One conspicuous hypothesis is abiogenesis, proposing that life emerged from non-living matter through a progression of substance responses. Another speculation is panspermia, which places that life on Earth started from extraterrestrial sources, for example, microorganisms hitching a ride on shooting stars.

The principal types of life were probable straightforward, single-celled living beings that arose around 3.5 to a long time back. These early living things, known as prokaryotes, missing the mark on core and other film bound organelles. More than great many years, they expanded into a heap of animal groups, preparing for the perplexing and various life we notice today.

The Advancement of Multicellularity:

A critical crossroads in transformative history happened with the development of multicellularity. Roughly 1.5 quite a while back, certain single-celled creatures started framing states, establishing the groundwork for the improvement of complicated multicellular life. This progress denoted a significant change in the association and intricacy of natural frameworks, prompting the development of green growth, parasites, and in the end, creatures.

Multicellularity achieved additional opportunities for specialization and participation among cells. Separated cell types took into account the division of work inside a living being, empowering the development of more complicated body plans and organ frameworks. This advancement set up for the unbelievable variety of life that would unfurl in the resulting parts of transformative history.

The Cambrian Blast:

The Cambrian Blast, roughly quite a while back, addresses a striking period in transformative history set apart by a fast expansion of perplexing multicellular life. During this generally short land stretch, an astounding cluster of new body plans and physical designs arose. The fossil record from the Cambrian Blast gives a preview of the beginning phases of significant creature phyla, including arthropods, mollusks, and chordates.

The variables driving the Cambrian Blast are as yet a subject of logical examination. Speculations range from ecological changes, for example, expanded oxygen levels, to hereditary advancements that worked with the improvement of more intricate body structures. No matter what the main thrusts, the Cambrian Blast laid the basis for the mind blowing variety of life that kept on developing over the resulting ages.

Vertebrate Development:

The development of vertebrates addresses a critical part in the narrative of life on The planet. The progress from spineless creatures to vertebrates denoted a pivotal achievement in the improvement of mind boggling organic entities. The earliest vertebrates were jawless fish that showed up around quite a while back. After some time, these crude fish broadened, bringing about the jawed fish and in the long run to the principal tetrapods — four-legged vertebrates equipped for living ashore.

The move from oceanic to earthbound conditions delivered new difficulties and amazing open doors. Transformations like appendages, lungs, and a solid skeleton prepared for the development of creatures of land and water, reptiles, and in the long run vertebrates. Each move toward vertebrate development mirrors a progression of developments that permitted creatures to take advantage of various environmental specialties and adjust to an evolving planet.

The Time of Reptiles and Dinosaurs:

The Mesozoic Time, frequently alluded to as the Period of Reptiles, saw the predominance of dinosaurs ashore and the development of other reptilian gatherings. Dinosaurs, with their different structures and sizes, managed earthly biological systems for a long period of time. The advancement of quills in some dinosaur ancestries, logical for protection or show, set up for the later development of birds.

Around quite a while back, a horrendous occasion, perhaps a space rock influence, prompted the mass elimination of dinosaurs and numerous different species. This occasion, known as the Cretaceous-Paleogene (K-Pg) annihilation, made ready for the ascent of warm blooded animals as the predominant land vertebrates. The overcomers of this termination occasion developed into a wide exhibit of structures, including the progenitors of current warm blooded creatures.

Mammalian Radiation and Variations:

The Cenozoic Time saw the dangerous radiation of warm blooded creatures into different biological specialties. From little, nighttime bug eaters to enormous herbivores and dominant hunters, well evolved creatures adjusted to a great many conditions. The advancement of particular highlights, for example, hooves for running, wings for flight, and complex dentition for differed eats less, permitted well evolved creatures to take advantage of different environmental jobs.

One of the characterizing elements of well evolved creatures is the advancement of live birth and mammary organs, empowering the sustenance and care of posterity. The advancement of placental vertebrates, described by longer incubation periods and more mind boggling placentas, added to the achievement and enhancement of this gathering.

Human Advancement:

The tale of human development is an enthralling story that traverses a long period of time. The earliest individuals from the hominin ancestry, like Ardipithecus and Australopithecus, were bipedal primates that lived in Africa around 4 to a long time back. The rise of the variety Homo, including species like Homo habilis and Homo erectus, denoted the utilization of apparatuses and the development of hominins past Africa.

The development of Homo sapiens, physically present day people, happened something like quite a while back. The improvement of perplexing language, culture, and high level device utilize recognized Homo sapiens from other hominin species. The capacity to adjust to different conditions, combined with complex social designs, permitted Homo sapiens to spread across the globe and become the prevailing species on The planet.

The Job of Annihilation Occasions:

All through developmental history, mass eradication occasions play had an essential impact in molding the direction of life. While these occasions bring about the deficiency of various species, they likewise set out open doors for new types of life to arise and expand. The "Large Five" mass annihilations, including the previously mentioned K-Pg termination, have been crucial in resetting the stage for transformative advancement.

The reasons for mass eradications shift, going from space rock influences and volcanic action to environmental change and maritime anoxia. Every elimination occasion makes a permanent imprint on the transformative course of events, molding the creation of environments and affecting the bearings that future development might take.

Transformations to Evolving Conditions:

Development is a continuous cycle driven by the unique interchange among creatures and their surroundings. As environments shift, territories change, and new natural specialties arise, species should adjust or confront eradication. The capacity to adjust to changing conditions is a sign of fruitful developmental techniques.

Regular choice goes about as the directing power in this cycle, leaning toward characteristics that present a regenerative benefit in a given climate. Variations can appear at different levels, from hereditary changes that modify actual qualities to conduct adjustments that improve endurance. The continuous investigation into the hereditary premise of transformation gives bits of knowledge into the systems basic developmental change.

Transformative Weapons contest and Coevolution:

The idea of a transformative weapons contest depicts the continuous rivalry between species to outcompete each other or stay away from predation. This unique communication drives the development of attributes like speed, cover, cautious instruments, and hostile techniques. The exemplary illustration of hunter prey connections mirrors the ceaseless battle for endurance and conceptive achievement.

Coevolution, a connected peculiarity, happens when at least two species impact each other's development. Models incorporate the coevolution between blooming plants and their pollinators, as well as the continuous weapons contest among hosts and parasites. Coevolution can prompt perplexing environmental connections and the advancement of particular transformations that benefit the two players.

Transformative Bits of knowledge from the Fossil Record:

The fossil record fills in as a window into the past, giving substantial proof of the life forms that once possessed Earth. Scientistss carefully concentrate on fossils to recreate the life systems, ways of behaving, and natural jobs of antiquated species. Fossilized bones, engravings, and follows left by life forms add to how we might interpret developmental advances and verifiable biodiversity.

Headways in innovation, like registered tomography (CT) examining and three-layered printing, have altered the area of fossil science. These instruments permit researchers to make point by point virtual models of fossils, empowering a more nuanced comprehension of wiped out creatures. The proceeded with investigation of fossil-rich stores all over the planet holds the commitment of uncovering new experiences into beforehand obscure parts of transformative history.

Transformative Formative Science (Evo-Devotional):

Transformative formative science, or Evo-Devotional, investigates the connections between hereditary changes and the improvement of physical designs all through developmental history. By contrasting the formative cycles of various living beings, researchers gain experiences into the hereditary instruments fundamental developmental changes.

The field of Evo-Devotional has uncovered the rationed hereditary tool compartment shared by assorted creatures, underscoring the key likenesses in the sub-atomic cycles administering improvement. Understanding how changes in quality guideline add to the advancement of assorted body plans and designs upgrades our grip of the systems driving developmental development.

Development in the Anthropocene:

The ongoing age, known as the Anthropocene, is described by the significant effect of human exercises in the world's environments and biodiversity. Human-actuated changes, for example, deforestation, contamination, environmental change, and the presentation of intrusive species, present uncommon difficulties for some species.

The quick speed of natural change in the Anthropocene has prompted worries about the capacity of species to adjust and develop because of these new tensions. A few animal varieties might confront termination, while others might go through quick versatile development. Understanding the developmental elements in this period is vital for illuminating preservation methodologies and moderating the adverse consequences of human exercises on worldwide biodiversity.

Protection Suggestions and the Significance of Figuring out Transformative History:

The investigation of developmental history has significant ramifications for protection science. As human exercises undermine the endurance of various species and biological systems, understanding the transformative cycles that have molded biodiversity becomes fundamental for viable protection procedures.

Transformative bits of knowledge can illuminate endeavors to save hereditary variety inside populaces, comprehend the versatile capability of species confronting natural changes, and recognize key characteristics that add to flexibility. Moderates use information on transformative history to focus on regions for assurance, plan renewed introduction projects, and carry out measures to relieve the effect of environment misfortune and discontinuity.

Instructive Importance:

The account of transformative history holds colossal instructive worth. Showing the standards of development cultivates logical proficiency and a more profound appreciation for the interconnectedness of every living thing. Developmental science gives a system to figuring out the variety of life, the cycles that shape it, and our place inside this immense embroidery of presence.

Instructive projects, historical centers, and effort drives assume an essential part in conveying the miracles of transformative history to people in general. By drawing in individuals with the dazzling accounts of old living things, developmental changes, and the continuous cycles of variation, teachers add to a more educated and earth cognizant society.

1.1 Tracing the evolutionary journey of lions and their ancestors.

The lion, with its superb mane and directing presence, remains as an image of solidarity and magnificence. However, behind the cutting edge lion's appealing disposition lies a transformative excursion that traverses a long period of time. Following the strides of lions and their predecessors uncovers a spellbinding story of variation, biological collaborations, and methods for surviving that have molded these wonderful hunters into the notable animals we perceive today.

The Early Precursors:

The transformative ancestry of lions, deductively known as Panthera leo, can be followed back to the family Felidae, which arose around quite a while back. The earliest predecessors of present day felines were little, flesh eating warm blooded creatures that possessed the forests and prairies of the antiquated world. These little felids, developing after some time, laid the preparation for the different feline species we notice today.

Around a long time back, the sort Panthera arose, denoting an essential move toward the development of large felines. This uniqueness set up for the improvement of the Pantherinae subfamily, which incorporates lions, tigers, panthers, and pumas. The developmental direction of this subfamily features the special variations that permitted these hunters to become dominant hunters in different environments.

Variations for a Ruthless Way of life:

The progress of lions and their predecessors as hunters lies in a set-up of variations finely tuned for a ruthless way of life. One of the characterizing elements of huge felines, including lions, is their retractable hooks. Not at all like numerous different warm blooded creatures, enormous felines can withdraw their paws when not being used, saving them sharp and prepared for hunting. This transformation is critical for keeping up with secrecy during pursuits and ambushing prey.

Another wonderful variation is their strong jaw structure and concentrated dentition. Lions have sharp, cutting teeth intended for tearing through tissue and strong jaws fit for conveying a deadly nibble. These variations are fundamental for repressing and consuming their prey effectively.

The development of binocular vision is one more key variation in the weapons store of large felines. Front aligned eyes give profundity discernment, permitting exact judgment of distances during pursuits and ambushes. This visual keenness adds to the progress of huge felines as covert trackers in different scenes.

Developmental Pathways:

The developmental pathways of lions and their progenitors have been molded by topographical and ecological variables. Various species inside the Pantherinae subfamily have adjusted to different natural surroundings, going from thick wildernesses to open savannahs. The advancement of particular characteristics mirrors the powerful transaction between these huge felines and their surroundings.

The Cavern Lion (Panthera leo spelaea): A wiped out subspecies of lion, the cavern lion, occupied Europe and Asia during the Pleistocene age. Adjusted to the cruel states of the last ice age, these lions were appropriate for hunting in chilly conditions. Their remaining parts, frequently tracked down saved in permafrost, give important bits of knowledge into the morphology and conduct of antiquated lions.

The American Lion (Panthera leo atrox): Meandering North and South America during the Pleistocene, the American lion was a considerable hunter. Regardless of its name, it's anything but an immediate progenitor of the cutting edge African lion. The American lion had unmistakable elements, including a vigorous form and a more limited mane contrasted with its African partners. Environment changes and changes in prey accessibility probably affected the advancement of this species.

The Eurasian Cavern Lion (Panthera leo spelaea): This wiped out lion species possessed pieces of Europe and Asia during the Pleistocene. Creative portrayals of this lion on cave walls, for example, those in the Chauvet Cavern in France, offer looks into the concurrence of early people and these magnificent hunters.

Social Construction and Agreeable Hunting:

One of the characterizing highlights of current lions is their social design. Dissimilar to numerous other enormous felines that are single trackers, lions are known for their gathering living, or sociality, in prides. The advancement of social designs in lions has likely been affected by different biological variables, including prey size, environment, and rivalry with different hunters.

The social design of lions normally rotates around prides drove by a predominant male, in spite of the fact that alliances of guys might shape in certain occurrences. Lionesses inside a pride are frequently firmly related, framing a helpful unit for hunting and raising posterity. This helpful hunting technique gives benefits in bringing down bigger prey and shielding regions against rival prides.

The advancement of sociality in lions highlights the flexibility of enormous felines to different biological specialties. It is a demonstration of the adaptability of their conduct collection in light of ecological difficulties and open doors.

The African Lion (Panthera leo):

The cutting edge African lion, Panthera leo, addresses the apex of the transformative excursion inside the Pantherinae subfamily. Disseminated across sub-Saharan Africa, African lions have adjusted to various natural surroundings, including savannahs, fields, and open forests. The transformative outcome of African lions is complicatedly connected to their capacity to flourish in different environments and their specialization as dominant hunters.

Developmental Variations of the African Lion:

Mane Improvement: Among the unmistakable elements of male African lions is the advancement of a great mane. The mane serves both a defensive and open capability. It safeguards the neck and throat during conflicts with rival guys and signals development and strength to possible mates and opponents.

Regional Way of behaving: Lions display regional way of behaving, stamping and protecting domains against gatecrashers. This conduct is critical for keeping up with admittance to assets, for example, prey, water sources, and appropriate denning destinations. The development of territoriality in lions mirrors the opposition for restricted assets and the need to get regions for raising posterity.

Regenerative Systems: The conceptive techniques of lions are finely tuned to guarantee the endurance of posterity in a difficult climate. Lionesses synchronize their estrous cycles inside a pride, prompting common mating occasions. This synchrony builds the possibilities of numerous lionesses conceiving an offspring around similar time, working with agreeable consideration and assurance of fledglings.

Hunting Procedures: African lions are known for their cooperative hunting strategies. While lionesses are the essential trackers, facilitated endeavors with guys improve the probability of fruitful kills. The development of gathering hunting methodologies has permitted lions to focus on an extensive variety of prey, from little warm blooded creatures to enormous herbivores.

Preservation Difficulties and Endeavors:

In spite of their long and fruitful developmental history, present day lions face various preservation challenges. Human exercises, including environment misfortune, poaching, and human-untamed life struggle, compromise lion populaces across Africa. The continuous difficulties highlight the significance of understanding the transformative setting of lions to foster successful protection systems.

Preservation endeavors frequently center around territory security, local area commitment, against poaching measures, and tending to the struggles among lions and neighborhood networks. The job of transformative variations, for example, the improvement of social designs and hunting methodologies, should be viewed as in preservation wanting to guarantee the drawn out endurance of these notable hunters.

Hereditary Experiences into Lion Development:

Progressions in sub-atomic hereditary qualities have given important bits of knowledge into the developmental history of lions. Hereditary examinations, including mitochondrial DNA investigation and entire genome sequencing, permit researchers to follow the connections among various lion populaces and grasp examples of hereditary variety.

Hereditary exploration has affirmed the presence of particular lion populaces, each with one of a kind hereditary marks. This data is fundamental for overseeing and moderating the hereditary variety of lion populaces, especially as divided living spaces and human exercises keep on influencing their normal reaches.

1.2 Comparative analysis with other big cat species.

The family Felidae incorporates a different cluster of huge feline species, each interestingly adjusted to its current circumstance. Similar investigation among these great hunters, including lions, tigers, panthers, pumas, and cheetahs, uncovers shared and particular attributes. This investigation gives experiences into the transformative variations that have permitted these famous cats to flourish in differed environments and face assorted difficulties.

Size and Morphology:

Size and morphology recognize each enormous feline species, adding to their exceptional personalities.

Lions, with vigorous forms and strong forequarters, display sexual dimorphism with guys exhibiting particular manes. Tigers, the biggest of the enormous felines, brag a gigantic, extended body and show sexual dimorphism, with guys being bigger. Panthers, known for flexibility and deftness, have slim, smoothed out bodies and rosette-designed coats. Panthers, stockier and more vigorous, succeed in swimming and frequently go after sea-going species. Cheetahs, thin and worked for speed, include tear stripes on their appearances and non-retractable hooks for foothold during rapid pursuits.

Environment and Geographic Reach:

The geographic dispersion of huge feline species is unpredictably connected to their favored environments, mirroring their versatile advancement.

Lions overwhelmingly occupy sub-Saharan Africa, exhibiting versatility in prairies, savannahs, and semi-dry areas. Tigers, local to Asia, possess assorted living spaces like woods, prairies, and mangrove swamps. Panthers exhibit surprising flexibility, dwelling in African savannahs to the thick woods of Asia. Pumas flourish in South American rainforests, with an unmistakable proclivity for water. Cheetahs favor open prairies and savannahs in Africa and Iran.

Social Construction and Conduct:

Social construction and conduct shift altogether among enormous feline species, molded by biological variables and transformative history.

Lions, one of a kind in their sociality, structure prides comprising of related females, their posterity, and a predominant male. Tigers, dominatingly singular, mark immense domains with fragrance markings to dissuade rivals. Panthers, to a great extent lone and regional, adjust to different conditions. Panthers are by and large single however may endure others in their domains. Cheetahs, frequently single, may frame little male alliances or free gatherings of females with fledglings.

Hunting Procedures and Diet:

Unmistakable hunting techniques and dietary inclinations further stress the versatility of huge feline species to their surroundings.

Lions are known for agreeable hunting, utilizing procedures like ambushes and composed assaults on huge herbivores. Tigers, single trackers, depend on secrecy and trap to get prey, with a different eating routine including deer and wild hog. Panthers, flexible trackers, tail and snare prey, frequently pulling it into trees for assurance. Panthers, strong trackers, snare from water or trees, conveying serious areas of strength for a to enter prey skulls or shells. Cheetahs, particular for speed, chase more modest ungulates with rapid pursuits.

Regenerative Procedures:

Regenerative procedures feature the transformations for guaranteeing the endurance of posterity inside each large feline species.

Lions show synchronized estrous cycles in prides, working with shared mating occasions and helpful consideration of whelps. Tigers, essentially singular, take part in brief mating cooperations. Panthers, with bigger male domains, have less successive experiences during mating. Pumas and cheetahs, however by and large singular, may briefly relate during mating.

Transformations to Explicit Conditions:

Transformations to explicit conditions highlight the developmental reactions of enormous feline species to different natural specialties.

Lions' flexibility is clear in their capacity to possess a scope of conditions, from meadows to savannahs. Tigers' jackets give great cover in different scenes, while their huge domains mirror a requirement for space. Panthers' versatility permits them to explore both normal and human-modified conditions. Pumas' proclivity for water and strong nibbles reflect specialization in rainforest and sea-going territories. Cheetahs' smoothed out bodies and non-retractable paws feature transformations for open fields and fast pursuits.

Protection Status and Dangers:

Analyzing the preservation status and dangers looked by each large feline species is pivotal for figuring out their ongoing difficulties.

Lions face territory misfortune, human-untamed life struggle, and declining prey populaces, prompting worries about their protection status. Tigers stand up to dangers like poaching, territory obliteration, and human infringement, especially in divided scenes. Panthers are versatile yet face dangers from territory misfortune, struggle with people, and unlawful exchange. Pumas face issues like natural surroundings annihilation and poaching, affecting their populaces. Cheetahs battle with natural surroundings misfortune, human-untamed life struggle, and low hereditary variety, presenting difficulties for their endurance.

Hereditary Experiences and Protection Suggestions:

Hereditary experiences into enormous feline species give significant data to preservation endeavors and grasping their transformative history.

Studies including mitochondrial DNA examination and entire genome sequencing uncover interesting hereditary marks inside unmistakable lion populaces. Hereditary variety contemplations are vital for the drawn out endurance of these species, particularly in divided territories. Preservation methodologies ought to coordinate hereditary bits of knowledge to protect the versatility and strength of large feline populaces.

1.3 Exploration of fossil evidence revealing cranial adaptations.

The investigation of fossil proof gives an intriguing look into the developmental history of different creatures, permitting researchers to unwind the secrets of transformation and endurance more than large number of years. Among the various parts of life structures, cranial transformations stand apart as basic marks of developmental changes.

Fossilized skulls and cranial designs offer priceless experiences into the assorted systems that life forms created to explore their surroundings, secure assets, and flourish despite changing natural tensions. In this investigation, we dive into the rich embroidery of fossil proof, uncovering the cranial transformations that have formed the course of development.

1. **Cranial Variations in Early Vertebrates:**
   The earliest vertebrates denoted a critical crossroads in transformative history, progressing from oceanic conditions to earthly life. Fossil proof from this time, around quite a while back, uncovers urgent cranial transformations that worked with this shift.
   Progress from Water to Land:
   Fossilized stays of early tetrapods, like Acanthostega and Ichthyostega, give experiences into the variations expected for earthbound life. Their skulls display a mix of fish-like and land and water proficient like elements, exhibiting the steady progress from water to land. Key cranial variations remember changes for the jaw structure and the improvement of solid, weight-bearing skulls for supporting the head in an earthbound climate.
   Breathing Transformations:
   Cranial transformations for breathing air became fundamental as vertebrates moved onto land. Fossil proof of momentary structures, as Tiktaalik roseae, uncovers adjustments in the skull and gill curves, demonstrating the improvement of designs that considered both sea-going and flying breath. This undeniable a huge move toward the development of creatures of land and water and, in the end, reptiles.

2. **The Ascent of Dinosaurs:**
   The Mesozoic Period saw the ascent of dinosaurs, a different gathering of reptiles that wandered the Earth for a long period of time. Cranial variations in different dinosaur ancestries give urgent bits of knowledge into their biological specialties and ways of behaving.
   Theropod Skulls:
   Theropod dinosaurs, known for their bipedal position and savage propensities, showed a scope of cranial variations. Fossils like those of Tyrannosaurus rex uncover hearty, serrated teeth and strong jaws adjusted for catching and consuming prey. The construction of the skull proposes an accentuation on a savage way of life, featuring the proficiency of their taking care of systems.
   Sauropod Skulls:
   Interestingly, herbivorous dinosaurs like sauropods, like Apatosaurus and Brachiosaurus, displayed cranial transformations for an alternate eating regimen. Their skulls highlighted stretched jaws with stake like teeth appropriate for stripping vegetation. The construction of sauropod skulls gave effective means to handling enormous volumes of plant material, underscoring their variation to herbivory.

3. **Avian Development and Flight:**

   The progress from non-avian dinosaurs to birds addresses perhaps of the most surprising part in transformative history. Fossil proof enlightens the cranial transformations that went with the advancement of flight.

   Skull Adjustments for Flight:

   Archaeopteryx, a momentary structure among dinosaurs and birds, features cranial variations demonstrative of its capacity to fly. The improvement of a lightweight skull with a nose and diminished teeth decreased in general head weight, adding to the streamlined effectiveness important for controlled flight. Ensuing avian fossils, for example, those of present day birds, display further cranial transformations for different taking care of systems and flight mechanics.

   Braincase Amplification:

   Fossils of morning people uncover an extension of the braincase, demonstrating expanded cerebrum size. This cranial variation probably assumed a critical part in the improvement of perplexing ways of behaving, high level tangible discernment, and the refinement of flight abilities. The development of a profoundly effective nose additionally worked with different taking care of techniques, adding to the outcome of avian genealogies.

4. **Mammalian Cranial Advancement:**

   The advancement of vertebrates is portrayed by critical cranial variations that have prompted the assorted exhibit of species we notice today. Fossil proof reveals insight into the changes from early mammalian progenitors to the immense scope of structures found in present day vertebrates.

   Dental Variations:

   Fossilized skulls of early vertebrates, like Morganucodon, uncover dental transformations that assumed a urgent part in their developmental achievement. The advancement of particular teeth, including molars and incisors, considered differed slims down, adding to the natural flexibility of early warm blooded animals.

   Over the long haul, different mammalian ancestries advanced explicit dental transformations fit to their particular ways of life and biological specialties.

   Encephalization and Skull Shape:

   The development of warm blooded animals is likewise set apart by encephalization, or the expansion in cerebrum size comparative with body size. Fossil proof from early well evolved creatures to current structures grandstands changes in the shape and construction of the skull related with cerebrum development. The improvement of a domed skull and an obvious cranial pit mirrors the transformative accentuation on higher mental capabilities, adding to the versatile outcome of vertebrates.

5. **Cranial Transformations in Hominins:**

   The transformative history of hominins, including people and their precursors, is portrayed by huge cranial variations that support the rise of one of a kind mental capacities and ways of behaving.

Mind Extension and Cranial Limit:

Fossilized skulls of early hominins, for example, Australopithecus and Homo habilis, display an expansion in cranial limit contrasted with before primates. The development of the braincase recommends progressions in mental capacities, including critical thinking, apparatus use, and social intricacy. Resulting hominin fossils, including those of Homo erectus and Homo sapiens, uncover further expansions in cranial limit, stressing the significance of encephalization in human advancement.

Facial Morphology and Discourse:

Cranial variations in hominins reach out to facial morphology, remembering changes for the design of the jaw, teeth, and nasal sections. Fossil proof recommends adjustments in these elements, matching with the advancement of discourse and language. The reshaping of the skull took into consideration the enunciation expected for complex vocalizations, a sign of human correspondence.

6. **Paleontological Procedures and Innovative Advances:**

The investigation of cranial transformations in the fossil record has been enormously upgraded by progressions in paleontological procedures and innovation.

Figured Tomography (CT) Examining:

CT checking permits non-horrendous imaging of fossilized skulls, giving definite interior designs and empowering specialists to remake the cranial life structures with extraordinary accuracy.

This innovation has been instrumental in concentrating on the complicated subtleties of wiped out species and figuring out the practical parts of cranial transformations.

Three-Layered (3D) Printing:

The utilization of 3D printing innovation to fossilized skulls empowers researchers to make actual imitations for additional investigation. This active methodology permits analysts to control, measure, and study cranial transformations in manners that were already unthinkable, improving comprehension we might interpret the structure and capability of antiquated skulls.

Chapter 2

External Cranial Features

The outside cranial elements of creatures comprise a striking embroidery of transformations, giving a window into their developmental past, biological jobs, and utilitarian methodologies. From the engineering of the skull to the perplexing subtleties of facial highlights, these outer qualities pass on an abundance of data about an organic entity's life history and biological specialty. In this far reaching investigation, we explore the different scene of outer cranial highlights, unwinding the importance implanted in bone and tissue across different species.

1. **The Life systems of the Skull:**
   The skull, a perplexing blend of cranial bones, fills in as the defensive fort for the cerebrum. Including front facing, parietal, transient, and occipital bones, the plan and design of these parts contribute not exclusively to defending the mind yet in addition offer experiences into the developmental variations of the creature. Furthermore, the cranial stitches, sinewy joints interfacing these bones, uncover designs that give data about the formative history and age of an example.

2. **Skull Morphology and Variation:**
   Skull morphology, a vital part of outside cranial highlights, appears in varieties like dolichocephalic (extended) and brachycephalic (short and expansive) structures. The length and width of the skull are not inconsistent; they reflect versatile techniques and reactions to natural elements. Skull morphology frequently corresponds with explicit environmental specialties, affecting a life form's capacity to explore its environmental elements and obtain assets. Moreover, a few animal varieties show cranial peaks or horns, outside structures vital to thermoregulation, species acknowledgment, and battle for predominance.

3. **Facial Elements and Variations:**
   Facial elements offer a nuanced comprehension of a life form's dietary propensities and versatile procedures. Dentition, the game plan and sort of teeth, fills

in as a solid mark of taking care of inclinations. Carnivores show sharp, pointed teeth for tearing tissue, while herbivores brag wide, level teeth for effective plant material handling. The length and state of a living being's gag are complicatedly connected to its taking care of propensities. Longer gags are frequently connected with brushing herbivores, though more limited gags are normal for carnivores adjusted for hunting.

Nasal designs likewise assume a vital part in a creature's respiratory capacities, with huge nasal openings found in species participated in high oxygen consuming movement.

4. **Eye Position and Transformations:**

   Eye situation on the skull is a crucial determinant of a creature's field of vision. The qualification among binocular and monocular vision is a characterizing highlight, with binocular vision beneficial for profundity discernment and normal in ruthless species. Besides, eye size and orbital arrangement offer experiences into an organic entity's action designs, with bigger eyes frequently characteristic of nighttime transformations.

5. **Ear Morphology and Hear-able Transformations:**

   The size and state of a creature's ears add to its hear-able capacities. Bigger ears are much of the time tracked down in species dependent on hear-able signs, like bats and a few primates. Outside ear structures, including pinnae, help in sound confinement and correspondence, exhibiting the complex transformations driven by tangible necessities.

6. **Horns, Tusks, and Show Designs:**

   Outside cranial elements reach out past simple useful necessities, embracing fancy and show structures. Horns and prongs, found in different species, fill needs going from guard to intraspecific contest and mate fascination. The size, shape, and stretching examples of these designs impart data about a singular's wellness and social standing. Sexual dimorphism frequently appears in the elaboration of these outer highlights, with guys commonly displaying bigger and more unpredictable designs than females.

7. **Dermatocranial Designs:**

   Certain species, especially reptiles and explicit well evolved creatures, present dermatocranial structures like scales, scutes, or hard plates on the outside surface of the skull. These outer elements add to defensive capabilities, thermoregulation, and act as species-explicit identifiers. The development of these designs features the different procedures living beings utilize for endurance and transformation.

8. **Human Cranial Highlights and Development:**

With regards to human development, outer cranial highlights offer an intriguing story of transformation and variety. Human facial elements, molded by a mix of hereditary, natural, and social variables, display impressive changeability across populaces. The investigation of skull morphology and facial attributes not just adds to how we might interpret human development yet in addition tracks down applications in legal human studies.

Besides, the human skull grandstands variations for bipedalism, including the remarkable situating of the foramen magnum, denoting a basic achievement in our transformative excursion.

2.1 Detailed examination of the lion's external skull structure.

The lion, Panthera leo, is a dominant hunter and a glorious individual from the Felidae family. Its outside skull structure fills in as a vital part in grasping its transformative variations, ruthless way of behaving, and environmental specialty. This point by point assessment plans to dive into different parts of the lion's skull morphology, revealing insight into its particular highlights and useful importance.

General Skull Morphology:

The lion's skull is an intricate construction that mirrors its flesh eating nature and savage way of life. The skull is strong and extended, displaying variations for strong gnawing and tearing. The conspicuous sagittal peak, a hard edge along the skull's midline, is a distinctive component, showing solid jaw muscles for quelling prey.

Cranial Highlights:

Looking at the lion's cranial highlights gives bits of knowledge into tangible variations. The eyes, situated on the facade of the skull, add to binocular vision, pivotal for profundity discernment during hunting. The generally little, adjusted ears help in sound limitation, working with the location of prey or expected dangers.

Dental Variations:

The lion's dentition is specific for a flesh eating diet, with sharp and vigorous teeth intended for catching, killing, and consuming prey. The canines are especially imposing, filling in as deadly weapons for holding and conveying a lethal chomp. The dental recipe of lions mirrors their predatory nature, with variations for shearing and tearing meat effectively.

Jaw Design:

The lion's jaw structure is a wonder of developmental transformation, empowering it to apply enormous power during taking care of and hunting. The strong jaw muscles, secured to the sagittal peak, consider areas of strength for a power, working with the utilization of bone and intense tissues. This transformation is vital for the lion's capacity to extricate supplements from its prey effectively.

Temporalis Muscle and Sagittal Peak:

The advancement of the temporalis muscle, answerable for jaw development, is unpredictably connected to the lion's sagittal peak.

The bigger the sagittal peak, the more powerful the temporalis muscle, featuring the connection between's skull morphology and the lion's ruthless way of life. This relationship is a demonstration of the transformative tensions that have molded the lion's skull after some time.

Mandible and Masticatory Muscles:

The lion's mandible, or lower jaw, is an essential part in its taking care of contraption. The hearty mandibular construction, combined with strong masticatory muscles, considers effective biting and handling of a predatory eating regimen. This variation adds to the lion's capacity to consume an extensive variety of prey, from more modest well evolved creatures to bigger ungulates.

Zygomatic Curve and Savage Variations:

The zygomatic curve, otherwise called the cheekbone, is a vital component in the lion's skull that improves its predatory capacities. This hard construction gives a stage to the connection of strong jaw muscles, considering intense gnawing and tearing. The lion's advanced zygomatic curve is a demonstration of its transformation as a considerable hunter in the African savannas.

Nasal Depression and Olfactory Variations:

While the lion's feeling of sight is urgent for hunting, its olfactory variations are similarly significant. The nasal cavity of the lion is moderately little contrasted with a few different hunters, demonstrating a dependence on vision as opposed to an exceptionally evolved feeling of smell. This specialization lines up with the lion's hunting technique, which frequently includes visual following of prey.

Foramen Magnum and Neck Muscle structure:

The place of the foramen magnum, the opening at the foundation of the skull through which the spinal string passes, offers bits of knowledge into the lion's stance and velocity. The forward direction of the foramen magnum lines up with the lion's bipedal position, stressing its nimbleness and ability during pursuits. Moreover, the neck muscular build, emphatically created to help the lion's gigantic head, assumes a urgent part in stifling prey and safeguarding region.

Skull Sexual Dimorphism:

Sexual dimorphism is apparent in the lion's outside skull structure, with guys for the most part showing bigger and more vigorous skulls contrasted with females. This dimorphism is connected to the cutthroat idea of guys for mating and domain. The size and strength of the skull in guys are intelligent of their job as defenders and pioneers inside the pride.

2.2 Significance of the mane in male lions and its cranial implications.

The lion (Panthera leo), known as the "lord of the wilderness," is a famous species with an unmistakable component that separates the guys - the grand mane. This thick development of hair surrounding the heads of mature guys isn't simply an image of majesty yet a complicated characteristic with significant ramifications for the lion's way of behaving, social elements, and, surprisingly, cranial transformations. This complete investigation expects to unwind the diverse meaning of the mane in male lions, digging into its transformative beginnings, biological jobs, and the complicated cranial variations related with its turn of events.

1. **Transformative Beginnings and Advancement of the Mane:**
   The development of the mane in male lions is a demonstration of the animal varieties' variation to its current circumstance and social construction. The mane starts to create as guys approach sexual development, regularly something like year and a half to two years old. This timing agrees with the lion's entrance into adulthood and the foundation of its job inside the pride.

   The advancement of the mane is firmly connected to hormonal changes, especially an expansion in testosterone levels. As guys mature, their bodies go through critical hormonal movements, prompting the development of facial and neck hair. The course of mane improvement is progressive, and its full magnificence is commonly achieved by the age of five or six years. The mane's tone and length can change among people, going from blonde to dull brown or dark, with the last option frequently connected with more elevated levels of testosterone.

2. **Social Importance and Strength:**
   The mane's most clear job lies in the social order of lion prides. An advanced and dim hued mane fills in as a visual mark of a male lion's development, wellbeing, and, thusly, its strength inside the pride. Perceptions in the wild reliably show that guys with noteworthy manes are bound to expect positions of authority, declaring strength over different guys and affecting pride elements.

   The mane's part in strength isn't restricted to intra-pride communications. In conflicts with rival prides or lone itinerant guys, the mane turns into an image of solidarity and virility. The size and murkiness of the mane can dissuade likely opponents, going about as a visual showcase of the singular's capacity to protect an area and secure assets.

3. **Mate Fascination and Regenerative Achievement:**
   The meaning of the mane reaches out past friendly strength, assuming a basic part in mate fascination and regenerative achievement. Lionesses inside a pride show a reasonable inclination for guys with lavish, dim manes. This inclination is connected to the impression of the mane as an indication of hereditary wellness and by and large wellbeing.

   With regards to mate choice, the mane turns into a physically chosen characteristic. Lions with advanced manes are more fruitful in drawing in mates, prompting expanded conceptive open doors. The hereditary connection between a strong mane and conceptive achievement highlights the developmental benefit related with this characteristic, as those with noteworthy manes pass on their qualities all the more successfully.

4. **Thermoregulation and Ecological Transformations:**
   Past its social and conceptive jobs, the mane serves reasonable capabilities connected with the lion's current circumstance. The African savanna, where lions prevalently live, is described by temperature limits, from singing intensity during the day to cooler evenings. The thick fur of the mane gives protection against these temperature varieties, adding to the lion's capacity to direct its internal heat level.

   During sweltering days, the mane's protection safeguards the lion from the sun's immediate beams, forestalling overheating. On the other hand, during cold evenings, the mane gives warmth, supporting the lion in keeping an agreeable internal heat level. This versatile component grandstands the complex harmony between transformative attributes and natural difficulties.

5. **Cranial Ramifications of Mane Improvement:**
   Understanding the cranial ramifications of mane improvement requires a point by point assessment of the lion's skull structure. The presence of the mane presents unmistakable variations in the hidden skeletal system, impacting different cranial highlights.

6. **Sagittal Peak and Testosterone Levels:**
   The sagittal peak, a hard edge along the skull's midline, is more articulated in guys with advanced manes. This peak fills in as a connection point for the temporalis muscle, which is liable for jaw development. The connection between's mane advancement and the sagittal peak is demonstrative of the job of testosterone in molding both the mane and the basic cranial designs.

   More significant levels of testosterone in dull maned guys contribute not exclusively to the development of the mane yet in addition to the improvement of a vigorous sagittal peak.

   This transformation improves the lion's gnawing strength, stressing the connection between sexual choice, social predominance, and cranial morphology.

7. **Cranial Sexual Dimorphism:**
   The presence of a mane presents sexual dimorphism in the lion's cranial construction. Male and female skulls show unmistakable contrasts, especially in districts related with mane advancement. These distinctions go past the shallow appearance of the mane and stretch out to the hidden variations important to help and support this striking component.

8. **Zygomatic Curve and Mane Backing:**
   The zygomatic curve, or cheekbone, in male lions with manes is much of the time more powerful contrasted with females. This transformation offers extra help for the heaviness of the mane, disseminating the heap uniformly and forestalling unjustifiable weight on the skull. The relationship between's the improvement of the zygomatic curve and the presence of a mane features the cranial transformations that go with this conspicuous component.

The vigorous zygomatic curve not just fills in as underlying scaffolding for the mane yet in addition adds to the lion's by and large cranial strength. This variation lines up with the utilitarian necessities of a hunter, especially one participated in ways of behaving related with strength and regional protection.

9. **Neck Muscular structure and Mane Backing:**

Supporting the weight and construction of the mane puts a significant burden on the neck muscular build of male lions. Accordingly, the neck muscles in guys with advanced manes are more strong contrasted with those in females. This variation is vital for supporting the mane, permitting guys to convey this element without undermining their nimbleness or by and large actual abilities.

The connection between's neck muscular structure and mane advancement features the coordinated idea of physiological and morphological variations. The strong neck muscles support the mane as well as add to the lion's capacity to take part in ways of behaving, for example, thundering, which is vital for correspondence inside and past the pride.

10. **Foramen Magnum and Mane-Related Stance:**

The place of the foramen magnum, the opening at the foundation of the skull through which the spinal line passes, is impacted by the advancement of the mane. The forward direction of the foramen magnum in male lions is adjusted to help the remarkable stance related with the presence of a mane.

Male lions with advanced manes frequently take on a more upstanding and forcing stance, highlighting their grand appearance. The forward position of the foramen magnum obliges this stance, stressing the interconnected idea of skeletal variations and social presentations related with the mane.

11. **Transformative Compromises:**

While the mane gives various benefits regarding social strength, mate fascination, and natural transformation, it likewise accompanies developmental compromises. The energy expected for mane advancement and support is significant, redirecting assets that could some way or another be distributed to different parts of the lion's physiology.

The obviousness of the mane can likewise make guys more noticeable to possible dangers, particularly during hunting. Developmental tensions have subsequently formed the harmony between the benefits and disservices of having a conspicuous mane, stressing the nuanced idea of regular determination and transformation.

12. **Preservation Suggestions:**

Understanding the meaning of the mane in male lions has suggestions for preservation endeavors. The safeguarding of this notorious characteristic is significant for keeping up with the species' normal ways of behaving, social elements, and regenerative achievement. Protectionists should consider the job of the mane in the species' environment while creating systems for the conservation of these great hunters.

Keeping up with hereditary variety, incorporating attributes related with the mane, is fundamental for the drawn out wellbeing of lion populaces. Preservation drives ought to expect to safeguard living spaces, alleviate human-untamed life clashes, and address factors that might upset the normal ways of behaving and transformations of lions, including those connected with the mane.

2.3 Adaptations for powerful biting and securing prey.

Dominant hunters, arranged at the zenith of their individual pecking orders, have developed a set-up of momentous variations to guarantee their endurance and accomplishment as trackers. Among these variations, the improvement of strong gnawing capacities is central for getting prey proficiently. This investigation dives into the complicated transformations found in dominant hunters, zeroing in on their cranial designs, dentition, and related muscular structure that add to their impressive gnawing ability.

1. **Cranial Designs and Jaw Life systems:**

The cranial designs of dominant hunters assume an essential part in working with strong gnawing. The skulls of these hunters are described by vigor, strength, and particular highlights that improve force transmission during gnawing. The vital components of their cranial life structures include:

1. **Sagittal Peak:**
   A conspicuous sagittal peak is much of the time present along the midline of the skull. This hard edge fills in as a connection site for strong jaw muscles, empowering proficient power age during gnawing. The sagittal peak is especially articulated in hunters that depend on a squashing or shearing chomp, like large felines and hyenas.
2. **Zygomatic Curve:**
   The zygomatic curve, or cheekbone, is an essential part of the hunter's skull. In dominant hunters, the zygomatic curve is hearty and gives a strong stage to the connection of gigantic temporalis muscles. These muscles are liable for jaw conclusion and assume a significant part in creating the power expected for strong nibbles.
3. **Mandible Construction:**

The mandible, or lower jaw, is one more basic component in the gnawing contraption of dominant hunters. It is adjusted for strength and solidness, permitting these hunters to endure the powers applied during gnawing. The mandibular symphysis, where the two parts of the mandible meet at the jawline, is frequently melded or very much supported to improve security during gnawing.

II. Dentition and Tooth Morphology:

Dentition in dominant hunters is exceptionally specific to oblige different hunting and taking care of procedures. The kinds of teeth, their course of action, and their particular morphologies add to the hunter's capacity to seize, immobilize, and process prey productively.

1. **Incisors:**

   While not the essential devices for killing, incisors in dominant hunters are adjusted for holding and tearing. In certain species, for example, large felines, the incisors are somewhat little yet sharp, supporting beginning control of prey.

2. **Canines:**

   Canines are the notorious weapons of dominant hunters, frequently stretched, sharp, and fit for conveying a deadly nibble. Canines serve different capabilities, including grasping and penetrating crucial areas of prey during an assault. In species like large felines, the retractable idea of their canines further improves their adequacy.

3. **Premolars and Molars:**

Premolars and molars are adjusted for cutting, shearing, and squashing. Carnivores regularly have edge like premolars that help with cutting through tissue, while molars are more vigorous and appropriate for squashing bones. These variations empower hunters to remove greatest sustenance from their prey.

III. Strong Transformations:

The viability of a strong nibble not entirely set in stone by the design of the skull and dentition but on the other hand is dependent upon the strength and coordination of the related muscular build.

1. **Temporalis Muscle:**

   The temporalis muscle is a central member in the gnawing component of dominant hunters. This muscle starts from the sagittal peak and embeds onto the mandible, considering strong jaw conclusion. In enormous hunters like huge felines, the temporalis muscle is extraordinarily evolved, empowering a powerful nibble essential for repressing prey.

2. **Masseter Muscle:**

   The masseter muscle, liable for the end of the jaw, is one more fundamental part of the gnawing contraption. It starts from the zygomatic curve and connects to the mandible, giving extra strength during jaw conclusion. In dominant hunters, the masseter muscle is powerful and all around adjusted for producing huge gnawing force.

3. Neck Muscular build:

The muscles of the neck are necessary to balancing out the head and working with exact control during gnawing. Dominant hunters, particularly those that participate in grappling with prey, have advanced neck muscular build. This variation improves their capacity to immobilize and control battling prey, forestalling escape.

IV. Gnawing Methodologies and Hunting Strategies:

Transformations for strong gnawing are intently attached to the hunting procedures and strategies utilized by dominant hunters. Various species have advanced remarkable ways to deal with secure prey successfully, mirroring their environmental specialties and transformative chronicles.

1. **Snare Hunters:**
   Species like huge felines frequently depend on secrecy and snare strategies. Their variations for strong gnawing line up with the need to curb prey rapidly and productively during shock assaults. The blend areas of strength for of muscles, sharp canines, and a very much planned gnawing system permits them to immobilize their quarry quickly.

2. **Pursuit Hunters:**
   Creatures that take part in pursuit hunting, for example, wolves and hyenas, show variations that help delayed pursues and actual cooperations with prey. The improvement of hearty neck muscles and a strong chomp is essential for these hunters to cut down bigger prey through sheer power and perseverance.

3. **Foragers:**

On account of scroungers like hyenas, transformations for strong gnawing are fundamental for getting to and handling intense corpses. Their dentition, particularly the devastating premolars and molars, permits them to break bones and concentrate important supplements from rummaged remains.

V. Environmental and Transformative Impacts:

The transformations for strong gnawing in dominant hunters are complicatedly connected to their environmental jobs and developmental narratives. The particular tensions forced by their surroundings, prey accessibility, and cooperations with different species have formed these transformations north of millions of years.

1. **Coevolution with Prey:**
   Hunters and their prey take part in a transformative weapons contest, prompting the improvement of variations and counter-variations. Dominant hunters, through regular determination, have refined their gnawing abilities to match the protective techniques of their prey. This coevolutionary dynamic has prompted the variety of gnawing transformations saw in various hunter prey connections.

2. **Specialty Specialization:**

The natural specialty involved by dominant hunters impacts the particular variations they create. For example, the variations of a crocodile, a semi-oceanic hunter, vary from those of an earthbound huge feline. The climate and accessible prey in their separate specialties have molded the advancement of their gnawing contraption.

VI. Preservation Suggestions:

Understanding the variations for strong gnawing in dominant hunters has suggestions for their protection. These transformations are finely tuned to the normal ways of behaving and natural jobs of these species. Protection endeavors ought to think about the safeguarding of environments that help different prey populaces, as well as the counteraction of elements that might disturb the coevolutionary connections among hunters and prey.

VII. Mechanical Applications:

Reading up the transformations for strong gnawing in dominant hunters has biological importance as well as down to earth applications. Experiences acquired from these variations can move the plan of biomimetic apparatuses and hardware. For instance, the design and mechanics of hunter jaws have impacted the improvement of proficient cutting apparatuses and clinical instruments.

Chapter 3

Internal Cranial Structures

The cranial designs of creatures are a wonder of natural designing, lodging and safeguarding quite possibly of the most fundamental organ - the cerebrum. This interior intricacy isn't just a consequence of transformative cycles yet in addition assumes an essential part in the working and endurance of living beings. This extensive investigation dives into the interior cranial designs, inspecting the complexities of the cerebrum, the supporting brain structures, and the vascular frameworks that add to the general working of the vertebrate head.

1. **The Mind: The Focal point of Brain Usefulness:**

The mind, an organ of unmatched intricacy, is the point of convergence of the inner cranial designs. Containing billions of neurons and a multifaceted organization of brain associations, the mind fills in as the war room for a creature's physiological and social capabilities.

1. **Significant Mind Areas:**
   Forebrain:
   The forebrain envelops the frontal cortex, thalamus, and nerve center. The frontal cortex, the biggest piece of the mind, is answerable for higher mental capabilities, tangible handling, and intentional engine exercises. The thalamus goes about as a hand-off place for tactile data, while the nerve center directs autonomic capabilities and assumes a vital part in the endocrine framework.
   Midbrain:
   The midbrain, or mesencephalon, fills in as an extension between the forebrain and hindbrain. It is engaged with hear-able and visual handling, as well as the guideline of engine capabilities.
   Hindbrain:
   The hindbrain comprises of the cerebellum, pons, and medulla oblongata.

The cerebellum facilitates engine developments and equilibrium, the pons aids correspondence between various cerebrum locales, and the medulla oblongata controls fundamental capabilities like heartbeat, breathing, and pulse.

2. **Hemispheric Specialization:**

In many vertebrates, particularly well evolved creatures, the mind is separated into two sides of the equator - the left and the right. Hemispheric specialization is noticed, where various capabilities are related with every half of the globe. For instance, in people, language handling is much of the time amassed in the left half of the globe, while spatial and visual handling is more unmistakable in the right side of the equator.

3. **Brain Pliancy:**

The cerebrum's capacity to adjust and rearrange itself because of encounters, known as brain versatility, is an entrancing part of its inner construction. Brain versatility takes into account learning, memory arrangement, and recuperation from wounds. The rebuilding of brain associations assumes an essential part in shaping an organic entity's way of behaving and reactions to its current circumstance.

II. Defensive Designs: The Skull and Meninges:

Encompassing the fragile cerebrum are defensive designs that shield it from mechanical harm and give a steady climate to ideal working. The head, a hard nook, and the meninges, an arrangement of films, cooperate to safeguard the cerebrum from outside powers.

1. **The Skull:**

The skull is the skeletal design that encases and safeguards the mind. Made out of bones like the front facing bone, parietal bones, worldly bones, and occipital bone, the noggin gives an unbending safeguard. The joint enunciations between these bones are known as stitches, and they meld over the long haul to make a strong, defensive nook.

2. **Meninges:**

The meninges are three layers of films that encompass the mind and spinal rope. These layers are, from furthest to deepest, the dura mater, arachnoid mater, and pia mater. The meninges give extra assurance, padding the cerebrum and spinal rope from shocks and effects. They likewise help contain and flow cerebrospinal liquid (CSF), which goes about as a safeguard and gives supplements to the cerebrum.

III. Vascular Framework: Guaranteeing Oxygen and Supplement Supply:

The cerebrum is a metabolically dynamic organ that requires a consistent and dependable inventory of oxygen and supplements. The vascular framework, containing courses, veins, and vessels, assumes a significant part in keeping up with this essential stock.

1. **Circle of Willis:**
   The Circle of Willis is a circulatory anastomosis that guarantees a constant blood supply to the mind, especially in case of blockages or breaks in blood stream. This round plan, framed by the joining of significant corridors, directs pulse and keeps a predictable progression of oxygenated blood to the mind.

2. **Blood-Cerebrum Obstruction:**
   The blood-cerebrum hindrance (BBB) is a specifically porous boundary that isolates the blood circling in the vessels from the extracellular liquid of the mind tissue. Made out of particular endothelial cells, the BBB keeps hurtful substances from entering the mind while permitting fundamental supplements and gases to go through. This obstruction is urgent for keeping up with the fragile biochemical equilibrium inside the mind.

3. **Cerebral Flow:**

Cerebral flow guarantees the conveyance of oxygen and supplements to the cerebrum's assorted districts. The many-sided organization of veins, including the front, center, and back cerebral conduits, supplies various region of the cerebrum with the assets they require. Cerebral dissemination is finely controlled to satisfy the powerful metabolic needs of different cerebrum districts.

IV. Brain Designs and Pathways: The Intricacy of Availability:
Inside the cerebrum, a huge organization of brain designs and pathways works with correspondence between various locales, considering composed reactions to boosts and the execution of complicated ways of behaving.

1. **Brain processes:**
   Brain processes are heaps of nerve filaments that send signals between various districts of the mind or between the cerebrum and different pieces of the body. Axons, the long projections of nerve cells, structure these pathways, making perplexing organizations that work with the transmission of electrical motivations and data handling.

2. **White Matter and Dark Matter:**
   The cerebrum is made out of white matter and dim matter. White matter basically comprises of myelinated axons, shaping the correspondence roadways between various cerebrum locales. Dim matter, wealthy in cell bodies and dendrites, is where data is handled and coordinated. The harmony among white and dark matter fluctuates across various mind structures, mirroring their individual capabilities.

3. **Limbic Framework:**
   The limbic framework, frequently alluded to as the close to home mind, assumes a urgent part in profound reactions, memory development, and learning. Parts like the hippocampus, amygdala, and nerve center are interconnected,

framing a mind boggling network that impacts both mental and profound parts of conduct.

4. **Corpus Callosum:**

The corpus callosum is a thick heap of nerve filaments that interfaces the left and right sides of the equator of the cerebrum. It empowers correspondence and coordination between the two halves of the globe, working with incorporated handling and reactions.

5. **Basal Ganglia:**

The basal ganglia, a gathering of cores arranged profound inside the cerebrum, are engaged with engine control, procedural learning, and mental capabilities. Messes influencing the basal ganglia can prompt development problems, underlining their essential job in arranging deliberate developments.

V. Tactile Handling Designs: From Discernment to Activity:

The interior cranial designs are unpredictably associated with tangible handling, permitting living beings to see their current circumstance, decipher boosts, and produce suitable reactions.

1. **Visual Handling:**

The occipital curves, situated at the rear of the cerebrum, are fundamentally liable for visual handling. The retina catches visual upgrades, and the optic nerve sends this data to the occipital curves, where it is deciphered, permitting organic entities to see and figure out the visual world.

2. **Hear-able Handling:**

The transient curves, situated on the sides of the mind, are urgent for hear-able handling. The hear-able cortex inside the fleeting curves deciphers signals from the ear, permitting organic entities to hear, perceive sounds, and answer hear-able boosts.

3. **Olfactory and Gustatory Handling:**

The olfactory bulb and gustatory cortex are answerable for handling scents and tastes, separately. These designs assume fundamental parts in food determination, aversion of unsafe substances, and the development of tangible recollections related with explicit scents and flavors.

4. **Somatosensory Handling:**

The somatosensory cortex, situated in the parietal curves, processes material data from the body's surface. It empowers living beings to see sensations like touch, strain, temperature, and agony, taking into account fitting engine reactions and cooperation with the climate.

VI. Endocrine Designs: Hormonal Guideline of Physiological Capabilities:

The endocrine framework, comprising of different organs and hormonal controllers, interfaces with the inward cranial designs to direct physiological capabilities and keep up with homeostasis.

1. **Pituitary Organ:**
   Arranged at the foundation of the mind, the pituitary organ is frequently alluded to as the expert organ. It secretes chemicals that direct other endocrine organs, affecting development, digestion, conceptive capabilities, and stress reactions.
2. **Pineal Organ:**
   The pineal organ, found profound inside the mind, produces melatonin, a chemical related with the guideline of circadian rhythms and rest wake cycles. Melatonin discharge is impacted by ecological light, featuring the perplexing association between inner designs and outside improvements.
3. **Nerve center:**

The nerve center, a little district at the foundation of the cerebrum, fills in as a pivotal connection between the sensory system and the endocrine framework. It produces chemicals that control the arrival of chemicals from the pituitary organ, arranging different physiological reactions, including internal heat level guideline, yearning, and thirst.

VII. Transformative Viewpoints: Following the Advancement of Inner Cranial Designs:

The interior cranial designs of vertebrates show momentous variety, mirroring the fluctuated developmental ways taken by various species. Relative life systems permits us to follow the development of these designs and comprehend the variations that have molded the vertebrate head more than huge number of years.

1. **Mind Size and Intricacy:**
   The development of the mind has seen a wonderful expansion in size and intricacy. From the moderately straightforward cerebrums of early vertebrates to the exceptionally tangled structures saw in well evolved creatures, the extension of the mind has been a main thrust in the development of mental capacities and versatile ways of behaving.
2. **Cranial Endocasts:**

Cranial endocasts, impressions or projects of the inner cerebrum depression, give important experiences into the minds of wiped out species. By contemplating these endocasts, researchers can surmise data about cerebrum size, construction, and expected mental capacities, offering a brief look into the neurological transformations of old living beings.

VIII. Pathologies and Issues: Unwinding the Secrets of Cerebrum Brokenness:

A comprehension of interior cranial designs is essential for translating the intricacies of mind related pathologies and problems. Conditions like neurodegenerative illnesses, awful mind wounds, and intrinsic issues frequently manifest through changes in the interior designs and elements of the cerebrum.

1. **Neurodegenerative Sicknesses:**
   Conditions like Alzheimer's sickness, Parkinson's infection, and Huntington's illness include moderate degeneration of brain structures. These sicknesses feature the weakness of explicit mind districts and the effect of underlying changes on mental and engine capabilities.
2. **Horrible Mind Wounds:**
   Horrible mind wounds result from outside powers affecting the head, prompting harm or interruption of interior designs. Understanding the outcomes of such wounds is critical for creating treatment techniques and recovery programs.
3. **Inborn Problems:**

Inborn problems influencing the cerebrum, for example, brain tube deformities, hydrocephalus, and hereditary anomalies, highlight the complicated transaction between hereditary elements and the advancement of inner cranial designs during undeveloped stages.

IX. Innovative Advances and Future Points of view:

Headways in innovation, for example, neuroimaging methods and sub-atomic science devices, have upset our capacity to concentrate on interior cranial designs.

These apparatuses give extraordinary experiences into the working of the cerebrum, considering symptomatic, remedial, and research applications.

1. **Neuroimaging Procedures:**
   Procedures like attractive reverberation imaging (X-ray), processed tomography (CT), and utilitarian X-ray (fMRI) empower harmless perception of interior cranial designs. These innovations have altogether progressed how we might interpret mind life systems, network, and utilitarian initiation designs.
2. **Sub-atomic and Cell Approaches:**
   Propels in atomic and cell science have permitted analysts to investigate the hereditary and cell components that underlie the turn of events and working of inside cranial designs. Methods, for example, quality altering and undifferentiated organism research offer promising roads for understanding and possibly controlling cerebrum capability.
3. **Cerebrum Machine Points of interaction:**

The improvement of cerebrum machine interfaces (BMIs) addresses a boondocks in neuroscience and innovation mix. BMIs permit direct correspondence between the cerebrum and outer gadgets, holding possible applications for neuroprosthetics, correspondence helps for people with loss of motion, and improved mental capabilities.

3.1In-depth analysis of the lion's internal cranial anatomy.

The lion (Panthera leo), frequently worshipped as the lord of the collective of animals, has an entrancing interior cranial life systems that is unpredictably associated with its ruthless way of life, social design, and developmental transformations. This far reaching examination dives into the inward universe of lions, disentangling the secrets of their interior cranial designs, brain processes, and vascular frameworks.

1. **The Defensive Stronghold: The Head and Meninges:**

1. **The Head:**

   At the center of the lion's inside cranial life structures lies the head, a hard fortification that typifies and safeguards the cerebrum from outside powers. Involving different bones, including the front facing, parietal, worldly, and occipital bones, the lion's head is a hearty construction intended for versatility. As in all vertebrates, the head's essential capability is to shield the mind, guaranteeing its security during the lion's dynamic and frequently dangerous way of life.

   The combination of these bones at stitches over the long run builds up the skull, making a tough and solid nook. The front facing bone structures the lion's brow, the parietal bones add to the upper skull, the fleeting bones house the ear structures, and the occipital bone structures the back and base of the skull.

   The multifaceted enunciation of these bones is a demonstration of the developmental cycles that have molded the lion's defensive cranial system.

2. **Meninges:**

The meninges, a tri-layered arrangement of films encompassing the cerebrum, add an extra layer of protection to the lion's inward cranial life structures. These layers, known as the dura mater, arachnoid mater, and pia mater, work in show to safeguard the cerebrum from shocks, effects, and expected wounds. The dura mater, the furthest layer, is an intense, stringy film that lines the internal surface of the skull, offering primary help. The arachnoid mater lies underneath the dura mater, and the sensitive pia mater sticks straightforwardly to the mind's surface.

The meninges serve a defensive job as well as add to the flow and control of cerebrospinal liquid (CSF). This reasonable, vapid liquid goes about as a pad, retaining shocks and giving lightness to the mind. Understanding the lion's meninges gives bits of knowledge into the fragile harmony among security and liquid elements inside the cranial hole.

II. The War room: Brain Designs and Pathways:

1. **Cerebral Life structures:**

   The lion's mind, the seat of its mental capacities and complex ways of behaving, is a work of art of transformative designing. The forebrain, midbrain, and hindbrain all in all coordinate the lion's tangible discernments, engine capabilities, and higher mental cycles.

Forebrain:

The forebrain, involving the frontal cortex, thalamus, and nerve center, overwhelms the lion's interior cranial scene. The frontal cortex, the biggest part, oversees progressed mental capabilities, tactile handling, and deliberate developments. The thalamus goes about as a hand-off station for tangible data, while the nerve center directs autonomic capabilities and endocrine reactions.

Midbrain:

Arranged between the forebrain and hindbrain, the midbrain is engaged with hear-able and visual handling. It frames a pivotal connection in the brain processes that work with the lion's capacity to answer upgrades in its current circumstance.

Hindbrain:

The hindbrain, including the cerebellum, pons, and medulla oblongata, is basic to the lion's coordination, balance, and imperative autonomic capabilities.

The cerebellum, with its complicated foliated structure, guarantees exact control of engine developments, improving the lion's readiness during chases and different exercises.

2. **Hemispheric Specialization:**

In the same way as other warm blooded animals, the lion's mind displays hemispheric specialization, where various capabilities are related with every side of the equator. This division of work empowers the lion to deal with data effectively and answer adaptively to its environmental elements. Viewpoints like regional mindfulness, social cooperations, and tangible insights are probable circulated across the sides of the equator, adding to the lion's generally mental capacities.

3. **Brain processes and Network:**

Inside the lion's mind, brain processes structure a complex organization that works with correspondence between various areas. Axons, the long projections of nerve cells, make these pathways, considering the transmission of electrical driving forces. The network inside the lion's cerebrum is pivotal for tactile reconciliation, engine coordination, and the execution of complicated ways of behaving fundamental for endurance and social communications.

III. Guaranteeing Imperative Assets: The Vascular Framework:

1. **Circle of Willis:**

The lion's vascular framework, involving courses, veins, and vessels, is central for providing oxygen and supplements to the cerebrum. The Circle of Willis, a circulatory anastomosis framed by the joining of significant corridors at the foundation of the mind, assumes a pivotal part in keeping up with constant blood stream. This round plan fills in as a shield, guaranteeing a consistent stock of oxygenated blood to the cerebrum even despite possible blockages or interferences.

2. **Blood-Mind Obstruction:**

   The blood-mind obstruction (BBB), a specifically penetrable hindrance, controls the section of substances between the circulatory system and the cerebrum tissue. This defensive component keeps hurtful substances from entering the mind while permitting fundamental supplements and gases to penetrate. The uprightness of the BBB is critical for keeping up with the lion's inner cranial climate and shielding the sensitive brain structures from expected poisons.

3. **Cerebral Flow:**

Cerebral flow in lions guarantees the conveyance of oxygen and supplements to various cerebrum locales. The front, center, and back cerebral conduits structure a complicated organization that provisions blood to explicit regions, supporting the different elements of the lion's cerebrum. The guideline of cerebral course is finely tuned to satisfy the unique metabolic needs of various brain areas.

IV. Tactile Handling Designs: Exploring the Climate:

1. **Visual Handling:**

   The lion's inner cranial designs are finely tuned for visual handling, lining up with its job as a talented hunter. The occipital curves, situated at the rear of the cerebrum, are principally liable for deciphering visual improvements. The retina catches visual data, and the optic nerve communicates these signs to the occipital curves, permitting the lion to see its current circumstance and execute exact visual errands basic for hunting and exploring its region.

2. **Hear-able and Olfactory Handling:**

   The lion's interior cranial life structures is prepared for handling hear-able and olfactory upgrades. The worldly curves, significant for hear-able handling, empower the lion to perceive and answer sounds in its current circumstance. Furthermore, the lion's advanced olfactory bulb and related structures add to its intense feeling of smell, assuming a crucial part in correspondence, domain stamping, and finding prey.

3. **Somatosensory Handling:**

The somatosensory cortex, situated in the parietal curves, processes material data from the lion's body surface. This handling permits the lion to see sensations like touch, strain, and temperature, giving significant input during social communications, prepping, and other proactive tasks.

V. Developmental Transformations: Following the Excursion Through Time:

The inward cranial life systems of lions bears the engravings of transformative cycles that have formed their methods for surviving north of millions of years. Near life systems, concentrating on the similitudes and contrasts with different felids and carnivores, divulges the particular variations that recognize the lion's inside cranial designs.

1. **Cranial Endocasts:**

Cranial endocasts, impressions or projects of the inward mind cavity, offer a brief look into the hereditary transformations of lions. These endocasts give important data about mind size, intricacy, and expected mental capacities, assisting researchers with deducing the transformative direction of the lion's interior cranial designs.

VI. Pathologies and Problems: Divulging Weaknesses:

The lion's inward cranial life systems, while strong and adjusted for endurance, isn't insusceptible to pathologies and problems. Awful cerebrum wounds, diseases, and intrinsic anomalies can influence the lion's brain structures, affecting its way of behaving, engine capabilities, and generally prosperity. Understanding these weaknesses adds to natural life preservation endeavors and the advancement of techniques to relieve wellbeing challenges in wild lion populaces.

VII. Preservation Suggestions: Safeguarding the Inner Sanctum:

Valuing the complexities of the lion's inner cranial life structures holds importance for protection endeavors. Saving the environments that help different prey populaces and limiting human-untamed life clashes are fundamental for guaranteeing the prosperity of lions and keeping up with the versatile trustworthiness of their inward cranial designs. Protection drives should consider the mind boggling exchange between the lion's science and its current circumstance to advance the drawn out endurance of this famous species.

3.2 Exploration of the brain size, structure, and its correlation with behavior.

The human mind, with its tremendous complexities and mental limits, has for some time been a subject of interest and request. The investigation of cerebrum size, structure, and its relationship with conduct is a multidisciplinary try that includes neurobiology, brain science, human studies, and transformative science. This extensive examination plans to unwind the secrets of neurological intricacy, looking at the connections between cerebrum morphology and the conduct collection showed by various species, with an emphasis on people.

1. **Cerebrum Size: A Measurement of Neurological Potential:**
1. **Encephalization Remainder:**
   Cerebrum size, frequently estimated comparable to body size, is a basic measurement known as the encephalization remainder (EQ). The EQ gives a normalized proportion of mind size that considers the normal cerebrum size for a creature

of a specific body size. This considers examinations across species and fills in as a sign of neurological potential.

In people, the EQ is uncommonly high, mirroring a surprising degree of encephalization contrasted with different vertebrates. This expansion in mind size has been related with the improvement of perplexing mental capacities, critical thinking abilities, and social ways of behaving that characterize human life.

2. **Allometry and Scaling:**

Allometry, the investigation of the connection between body size and other physical qualities, assumes a pivotal part in understanding the scaling of mind size. As living beings advance and change in size, the cerebrum's design should adjust to keep up with utilitarian effectiveness. Perceptions across species uncover that cerebrum size doesn't increment straightly with body size; rather, it follows a scaling relationship that is dependent upon specific tensions and transformative powers.

II. Cerebrum Construction: Intricacy Past Size:

1. **Dim Matter and White Matter:**
The mind's inward construction comprises of dark matter and white matter. Dim matter, made out of neuron cell bodies and dendrites, is liable for data handling and calculation. White matter, comprised of myelinated axons, frames the correspondence interstates that work with the transmission of signs between various cerebrum locales. The unpredictable harmony among dark and white matter is significant for the mind's general working.

2. **Cortical Collapsing:**
The human mind is portrayed by its exceptionally collapsed cerebral cortex, an element known as gyrencephaly. The collapsing of the cortex expands its surface region, considering a more noteworthy number of neurons and neurotransmitters. This cortical collapsing is especially articulated in people and certain other profoundly smart well evolved creatures, adding to the extended mental abilities saw in these species.

3. **Subcortical Designs:**

Past the cerebral cortex, subcortical designs like the hippocampus, amygdala, thalamus, and basal ganglia assume fundamental parts in different mental and close to home capabilities. The hippocampus is related with memory arrangement, the amygdala with close to home handling, the thalamus with tactile transfer, and the basal ganglia with engine control and procedural learning. The interchange among cortical and subcortical designs adds to the intricacy of conduct showed by creatures.

III. Connection with Conduct: Exploring the Social Scene:

1. **Mental Capacities:**
   The relationship between's cerebrum size and mental capacities is clear across species. In people, the development of the prefrontal cortex, a locale related with chief capabilities and navigation, is connected to cutting edge mental capacities, for example, thinking, critical thinking, and anticipating what's to come. The improvement of an enormous and complex cerebrum has empowered people to display a scope of mental abilities that support their innovative, phonetic, and social accomplishments.

2. **Social Intricacy:**
   Cerebrum size and construction are firmly connected to social intricacy in creatures. Species with bigger minds, especially an extended neocortex, frequently show more unpredictable social designs and ways of behaving. The neocortex, liable for higher-request mental capabilities, is remembered to assume a key part in handling social data and overseeing complex social connections. People, with their especially evolved neocortex, take part in complex social associations, collaboration, and correspondence that add to the wealth of human social orders.

3. **Apparatus Use and Development:**
   The connection between's mind size and device use is apparent in different species, including primates and certain bird species. The capacity to utilize devices requires progressed mental capacities, for example, critical thinking, arranging, and figuring out circumstances and logical results connections. Cerebrum structures related with these mental capabilities, like the cerebrum, are many times more created in species that display apparatus use.

4. **Rummaging Procedures:**
   Mind size and design are unpredictably connected to the searching techniques utilized by various species. In primates, for instance, species with bigger minds are frequently connected with more adaptable scrounging ways of behaving, permitting them to adjust to various natural specialties and food sources. This adaptability is credited to the mental cycles related with bigger minds, empowering life forms to actually explore and take advantage of their surroundings.

5. **Correspondence and Language:**

The advancement of language in people is intently attached to mind size and construction. The improvement of language includes complicated brain processes that require a very much planned interchange of different cerebrum locales, including those liable for hear-able handling, engine control, and higher-request cognizance. The relationship between's cerebrum size and etymological capacities highlights the job of neuroanatomy in molding the intricacy of human correspondence.

IV. Relative Examination Across Species:

1. **Incredible Gorillas:**
   Relative examination across primates, especially extraordinary gorillas, uncovers fascinating examples with regards to cerebrum size and design. While people possess the biggest intellect among primates, the extraordinary primates, including chimpanzees, bonobos, gorillas, and orangutans, likewise display varieties in mind size and intricacy. These varieties are related with contrasts in environmental specialties, social designs, and conduct variations inside the primate request.

2. **Cetaceans:**
   Cetaceans, like dolphins and whales, present one more charming instance of enormous brained organic entities. Regardless of their non-mammalian family line, cetaceans possess developed enormous brainpower that rival those of extraordinary primates concerning relative size. The improvement of perplexing correspondence frameworks, social designs, and critical thinking skills in cetaceans features the connection between's cerebrum size and refined ways of behaving in oceanic conditions.

3. **Birds:**

Birds, especially certain types of corvids and parrots, challenge the mammalian-driven perspective on cerebrum conduct connections. These avian species show striking mental capacities, critical thinking abilities, and instrument use regardless of possessing intellect with unexpected primary association in comparison to warm blooded animals. The concurrent development of perplexing ways of behaving in birds and warm blooded animals highlights the flexibility of mind designs to different natural and transformative tensions.

V. Developmental Points of view: Transformations and Particular Tensions:

1. **Social Mind Speculation:**
   The Social Mind Speculation suggests that the intricacy of social designs and connections in an animal groups is a main impetus behind the development of bigger cerebrums. Species that take part in complex social connections, agreeable ways of behaving, and complicated correspondence are remembered to encounter specific tensions leaning toward expanded mind size and mental capacities. This speculation makes sense of the varieties in cerebrum size and design saw across various species with particular social associations.

2. **Biological Difficulties:**

Variations to explicit natural difficulties likewise impact mind size and design. Species confronting mind boggling and variable conditions might advance bigger cerebrums to actually explore and take advantage of their environmental elements. The capacity to gain from encounters, display adaptable ways of behaving, and adjust to changing circumstances becomes beneficial in conditions where asset accessibility and difficulties vary.

VI. Brain adaptability: The Powerful Idea of the Mind Conduct Relationship:

Brain adaptability, the mind's capacity to rearrange itself because of encounters and natural improvements, adds a layer of intricacy to the cerebrum conduct relationship. The design and capability of the mind are not fixed; they can be impacted by learning, openness to new improvements, and versatile reactions to challenges. This unique nature of the mind permits creatures to adjust their conduct in view of evolving conditions, adding to their endurance and outcome in different conditions.

VII. Cerebrum Problems and Irregularities: Experiences into Ordinary Working:

Concentrating on cerebrum issues and irregularities gives significant bits of knowledge into the ordinary working of the mind. Conditions, for example, neuro-developmental messes, neurodegenerative sicknesses, and mental problems frequently include modifications in cerebrum construction and capability. Understanding these peculiarities adds as far as anyone is concerned of the perplexing connections between mind morphology and conduct.

3.3 Examination of sensory adaptations, including vision and olfaction.

Tactile transformations are essential to the endurance and outcome of life forms in their surroundings. The many-sided manners by which living beings see and cooperate with their environmental factors give significant bits of knowledge into the transformative cycles that have formed their tactile frameworks. Among the heap tangible variations, vision and olfaction stand apart as fundamental systems that contribute essentially to a life form's capacity to explore, find assets, and impart. This assessment dives into the interesting universe of tactile variations, zeroing in on the wonderful abilities of vision and olfaction.

1. **Vision: A Window to the World**
1. **Photoreceptor Specialization:**

    Vision, a tactile methodology that depends on the identification of light, has gone through different variations across species. One of the key transformations is the specialization of photoreceptor cells in the eyes.

    Various creatures display varieties in the sorts of photoreceptors, including poles and cones, and the dissemination of these cells on the retina.

    Bars: Dominating in low-light circumstances, poles are exceptionally delicate to light and are urgent for night vision. Nighttime creatures, like owls and felines, have a higher thickness of bars to upgrade their capacity to see in faint lighting.

    Cones: Cones, then again, are answerable for variety vision and capability best in brilliant light. Diurnal creatures, similar to people and many birds, have a higher thickness of cones, permitting them to see a more extensive range of varieties and explore in sufficiently bright conditions.

2. **Field of View and Binocular Vision:**
   The field of view is one more basic part of vision that shifts among species in light of their natural necessities. Creatures with an all encompassing field of view, similar to herbivores, can distinguish hunters from different points. Hunters, interestingly, frequently have front oriented eyes, giving a level of binocular vision that upgrades profundity insight and works with exact distance assessment while following prey.

3. **Variety Vision:**

Variety vision, an exceptional variation, empowers life forms to recognize various frequencies of light. While certain species, similar to canines, have dichromatic vision (seeing two essential tones), others, including people and many primates, show trichromatic vision, permitting them to see a more extensive range of varieties. This variation is especially profitable for errands, for example, distinguishing ready organic products, choosing mates, and knowing expected dangers.

II. Olfaction: Exploring the World Through Fragrances

1. **Olfactory Receptor Variety:**
   Olfaction, or the feeling of smell, is an amazing asset utilized by numerous organic entities for correspondence, route, and finding assets. The olfactory framework is described by a huge range of olfactory receptors that recognize explicit smell particles. The variety of these receptors adds to a creature's capacity to perceive many fragrances.

   Pheromone Recognition: Numerous creatures, including bugs and warm blooded animals, use pheromones — compound signs delivered into the climate — to speak with conspecifics. The specialization of olfactory receptors empowers the identification of pheromones, working with significant ways of behaving, for example, mating, an area stamping, and social holding.

   Fragrance Segregation: Certain species, similar to canines, are famous for their uncommon olfactory abilities. Canines have countless olfactory receptors, permitting them to separate between different fragrances with momentous accuracy. This variation has made canines priceless for undertakings like following, search and salvage, and recognition of booty.

2. **Vomeronasal Organ (VNO):**
   In certain species, the vomeronasal organ (VNO) assumes a vital part in identifying pheromones and other compound signals. While the VNO is well-developed in numerous vertebrates, including rodents and certain reptiles, its importance differs among species. The VNO upgrades the responsiveness of the olfactory framework to explicit substance signals, adding to social and regenerative ways of behaving.

3. **Olfactory Bulb Size and Mind Availability:**

The size of the olfactory bulb, the cerebrum area liable for handling olfactory data, is characteristic of a living being's dependence on its feeling of smell. Species with bigger olfactory bulbs frequently show increased olfactory awareness. The network of the olfactory bulb to other mind areas, for example, those related with memory and feelings, further highlights the complex job of olfaction in shaping way of behaving.

III. Near Points of view and Environmental Importance

1. **Transformations to Natural Specialties:**
   Tangible variations in vision and olfaction are complicatedly connected to the environmental specialties possessed by various species. Nighttime creatures, like bats and moths, have developed clear line of sight and olfactory variations that upgrade their capacity to explore and find prey in low-light circumstances. In the interim, marine warm blooded animals, similar to whales and dolphins, exhibit olfactory transformations fit to their sea-going conditions, depending more on echolocation and sound correspondence than olfaction.

2. **Hunter Prey Elements:**

The tactile variations of hunters and prey frequently take part in a transformative weapons contest. Hunters foster techniques to improve their hunting ability, while prey species advance systems to sidestep discovery. This powerful exchange between tactile variations adds to the equilibrium of hunter prey elements in assorted biological systems.

Chapter 4

Functionality Of The Jaw and Teeth

The jaw and teeth structure a noteworthy biomechanical gathering that lies at the core of vertebrate life systems. This complete investigation digs into the complexities of the usefulness, transformative variations, and different jobs played by the jaw and teeth across species. From the basic design of the jaw to the heap variations found in teeth, this assessment tries to disentangle the complicated transaction among structure and capability in the captivating domain of craniodental life systems.

1. **Craniodental Morphology: The Design Accuracy of Gnawing and Biting**
   The craniodental framework addresses a many-sided building configuration up-graded for the requesting undertakings of gnawing, biting, and handling different kinds of food. The design incorporates the mandible and maxilla, shaping the lower and upper jaws, individually.
   The mandible, a hearty bone, explains with the skull, offering help for the teeth and filling in as the essential anchor for the muscles associated with biting. Its portability and verbalization take into consideration a great many developments fundamental for effective rumination. Supplementing the mandible, the maxilla frames the upper dental curve, offering extra help and strength for the teeth.
   Teeth, the useful parts of the craniodental framework, show a different scope of designs. The tooth crown, the noticeable part over the gumline, shifts in shape and surface highlights, like cusps, edges, and depressions. The tooth root secures the tooth inside the jawbone, giving steadiness and backing during gnawing and biting. The arrangement of upper and lower teeth, known as dental impedi-ment, is vital for powerful rumination, with various species displaying explicit occlusal designs customized to their dietary requirements.
2. **Developmental Variations: An Embroidery of Dental Variety**
   Development has woven a rich embroidery of dental variations, mirroring the biological specialties and dietary inclinations of different species. Dental formu-lae, addressing the numeric plan of tooth types, offer bits of knowledge into the

developmental transformations across various living beings.

Heterodonty, the presence of various sorts of teeth, is a broad variation saw in well evolved creatures. Incisors, canines, premolars, and molars serve particular capabilities in handling food. The transformative procedure of heterodonty permits well evolved creatures to proficiently deal with an assortment of food things in light of their dietary prerequisites.

Then again, homodonty, where all teeth are comparable in structure and capability, is seen in specific reptiles and creatures of land and water. This transformation lines up with explicit taking care of techniques, like getting a handle on or penetrating, where teeth fill a more summed up need.

Warm blooded creatures, with their unmatched variety, exhibit a variety of dental variations. Carnivores have particular teeth for catching and consuming prey, including sharp canines for penetrating and carnassial teeth for shearing. Herbivores, adjusted to a plant-based diet, show teeth appropriate for crushing and handling sinewy vegetation, frequently highlighting wide molars for biting and cutting incisors for editing. Omnivores, with adaptable eating regimens incorporating both plant and creature matter, frequently display a mix of tooth types, exhibiting their flexibility.

Tooth substitution is a key transformation guaranteeing the nonstop usefulness of the dentition. Polyphyodonty, seen in non-mammalian vertebrates, considers the consistent substitution of teeth all through an organic entity's life. Conversely, diphyodonty, saw in warm blooded creatures, includes the consecutive substitution of deciduous (milk) teeth with long-lasting teeth, adjusting the requirement for utilitarian teeth in early life and long haul sturdiness.

3. **Practical Variety: Gnawing, Crushing, and Concentrated Variations**

The usefulness of the jaw and teeth stretches out past a simple biting device, integrating particular transformations for different environmental jobs.

Flesh eating species exhibit exceptional transformations designed for catching, repressing, and consuming prey. Canine teeth, frequently amplified and sharp, act as considerable weapons for seizing and penetrating. The length and heartiness of canines fluctuate among carnivores, mirroring their hunting methodologies and prey inclinations. Also, carnassial teeth, especially noticeable in felids and canids, structure scissor-like edges improved for shearing through meat, underlining the savage way of life.

Herbivores, adjusted to an eating routine wealthy in plant material, display particular variations customized for effective handling of sinewy vegetation. Dental batteries, found in species like ponies and rodents, comprise of columns of molars with level surfaces, working with the crushing and pulverizing of extreme plant strands. The dental morphology of herbivores is much of the time portrayed by a blend of wide, level molars for biting and cutting incisors for editing vegetation.

Omnivores, occupying a dietary specialty that incorporates both plant and creature matter, have flexible dental variations. The mix of incisors, canines, premolars, and molars permits omnivores to handle an extensive variety of food things. This versatility lines up with their pioneering taking care of conduct and the need to consume assorted dietary assets proficiently.

4. **Useful Elements: The Biomechanics of Gnawing and Biting**

The biomechanics of gnawing and biting include a planned exchange between the jaw, teeth, and related muscular build. The temporomandibular joint (TMJ), where the mandible verbalizes with the skull, is a pivotal part in working with the different developments expected for rumination.

Gnawing includes the underlying getting a handle on and cutting of food utilizing the incisors and canines. The gnawing force produced is affected by variables, for example, tooth morphology, jaw muscle strength, and the effectiveness of the temporomandibular joint. Carnivores frequently apply significant gnawing powers with their specific teeth, taking into consideration productive prey catch.

Biting, the ensuing crushing and pulverizing of food, transcendently happens in the molar area. The occlusal surfaces of molars, adjusted for explicit dietary requirements, interlock during biting to separate food into more modest, absorbable particles. The intricacy of biting examples changes among species, mirroring their taking care of systems and environmental jobs.

The jaw muscles, including the temporalis and masseter muscles, assume a crucial part in producing the power expected for gnawing and biting. The effectiveness of these muscles is intently attached to the variations in craniodental morphology, guaranteeing the useful uprightness of the whole framework.

5. **Dental Wear and Upkeep: A Long lasting Excursion**

Dental wear is an inescapable part of a creature's life, mirroring the steady utilization and mechanical burdens applied on teeth during gnawing and biting. The rate and example of dental wear give significant experiences into a living being's dietary propensities and age.

Carnivores, with their accentuation on tearing and shearing, frequently display explicit wear designs on their teeth. Wear features, coming about because of the contact between restricting teeth during impediment, can be demonstrative of the sorts of food handled and the power applied during gnawing.

Herbivores, participated in broad biting of sinewy plant material, may encounter wear designs related with the crushing and smashing of extreme vegetation. The advancement of complex occlusal surfaces on molars reflects variations to explicit dietary specialties and the requirement for effective food handling.

Dental upkeep is a powerful interaction including tooth emission, substitution, and ceaseless variation to the mechanical burdens forced during taking care of.

The capacity to keep up with utilitarian teeth all through an organic entity's life is essential for its endurance and regenerative achievement.

6. **Transformative Importance: A Continuous Adventure of Variation and Endurance**

The usefulness of the jaw and teeth is profoundly interlaced with the developmental achievement and natural specialty inhabitance of various species. The versatile radiation of well evolved creatures, set apart by the expansion of dental structures and works, mirrors the particular tensions forced by changed conditions and environmental difficulties.

The advancement of particular dental transformations lines up with the natural jobs played by various species. In the weapons contest among hunters and prey, the advancement of rapacious variations, for example, lengthened canines and carnassial teeth, has been significant for the progress of flesh eating ancestries. Alternately, herbivores have developed dental designs that empower proficient handling of plant material, displaying the coevolutionary elements among organic entities and their surroundings.

The fossil record fills in as a pivotal chronicle of developmental changes in craniodental morphology. Near investigations of fossilized teeth give experiences into the dietary inclinations, natural variations, and transformative directions of wiped out species. Tooth morphology has been instrumental in unwinding the connections between various taxa and understanding the environmental specialties they involved.

4.1 Understanding the powerful bite force of lions.

The lion, Panthera leo, remains as a notorious image of force and greatness in the set of all animals. One of the key ascribes adding to the lion's imposing status is its strong chomp force. This investigation dives into the physical and physiological parts of a lion's chomp, unwinding the components that make it one of the most intense nibbles among enormous felines.

1. **Craniodental Life systems: The Underpinning of an Imposing Nibble**
1. **Jaw Construction:**
   At the center of the lion's strong nibble is its hearty craniodental life structures. The lion's jaw structure, including the mandible and maxilla, is explicitly adjusted for creating and enduring enormous powers. The mandible, or lower jaw, is described by tough bone thickness and an articulated rakish interaction, giving areas of strength for an arm to the strong jaw-shutting muscles.
2. **Tooth Morphology:**

The lion's dentition assumes a critical part in its gnawing capacities. The plan of teeth in the upper and lower jaws incorporates incisors, canines, premolars, and molars. Nonetheless, the canine teeth especially hang out with regards to nibble force. The lion's canines are prolonged, sharp, and powerful, filling in as considerable weapons for catching, curbing, and consuming prey.

II. Nibble Power Estimation: Measuring the Power

1. **Logical Investigations:**
   Logical endeavors to comprehend and evaluate the chomp power of lions have been attempted through different investigations. These examinations utilize modern strategies, for example, chomp force meters and computational models, to gauge and reenact the power produced during a lion's nibble.

2. **Nibble Power Correlation:**

Lions are famous for having one of the most grounded chomp powers among enormous felines. Relative investigations uncover that the lion's chomp force is outperformed exclusively by the tiger among felids. The lion's nibble force is assessed to be around 650 pounds for each square inch (psi), exhibiting its outstanding craniodental transformations for strong gnawing.

III. Useful Elements: The Mechanics of a Lion's Chomp

1. **Gnawing Method:**
   The mechanics of a lion's chomp include a blend of physical variations and exact gnawing procedures. Lions utilize a stifling chomp to repress and kill their prey, focusing on the weak regions like the throat and neck. The long canines assume a critical part in entering profound into the prey's tissue, considering a powerful chomp and grasp.

2. **Shutting System:**

The end system of a lion's jaw is worked with by strong muscles, including the temporalis and masseter muscles. These muscles give the important power to close the jaw with wonderful speed and strength. The organized activity of these muscles adds to the proficiency of the lion's gnawing strategy.

IV. Environmental Importance: The Job of Nibble Power in Ruthless Systems

1. **Ruthless Variations:**
   The strong nibble power of lions is fundamental to their savage variations and hunting systems. Lions are dominant hunters, depending on their solidarity and composed bunch hunting methods to cut down enormous herbivores.
   The blend of a strong chomp and social collaboration inside prides improves the effectiveness and outcome of lion chases.

2. **Prey Oppression:**
   The lion's nibble is a vital instrument for enslaving prey. When a lion has caught its objective, the imposing chomp force becomes possibly the most

important factor, permitting the lion to apply command over the prey. The stifling nibble immobilizes the prey as well as helps in the resulting utilization process.

V. Transformative Setting: Nibble Power as a Versatile Benefit

1. **Coevolution with Prey:**
   The development of a strong nibble force in lions is complicatedly connected to their coevolution with prey species. As lions adjusted to become talented hunters, their prey at the same time created guarded systems. The development of a strong nibble force in lions should be visible as a reaction to the requirement for conquering prey transformations, making a unique transaction in hunter prey connections.

2. **Transformative Compromises:**

   The development of a strong chomp force includes compromises regarding energy consumption and physical transformations. The improvement of solid jaw muscles and powerful dentition requires huge energy assets, which lions obtain through their dietary decisions and hunting achievement. Transformative tensions have inclined toward those people with the physical elements helpful for creating strong nibbles, adding to the general wellness of the species.

VI. Neurotic Experiences: Difficulties to Chomp Power and Dental Wellbeing

1. **Dental Pathologies:**
   While a lion's chomp is an imposing weapon, it isn't safe to dental pathologies and difficulties. Dental issues, for example, tooth cracks, contaminations, and wear, can think twice about lion's nibble force. These pathologies might result from factors like age, wounds supported during hunting or regional debates, and the general strength of the singular lion.

2. **Suggestions for Endurance:**

   Dental wellbeing and the support of a strong nibble force are basic for a lion's endurance. The capacity to catch and consume prey straightforwardly impacts a singular lion's wellness and conceptive achievement. Lions with compromised nibble powers might confront difficulties in getting prey, possibly affecting their general wellbeing and endurance.

VII. Preservation Contemplations: Nibble Power in Wild and Hostage Conditions

1. **Territory and Prey Elements:**
   In the wild, a lion's chomp force is intently attached to its natural

surroundings and the elements of accessible prey. Protection endeavors pointed toward saving lion populaces should think about the biological variables that impact their savage ways of behaving. Living space protection, the accessibility of regular prey, and limiting human-untamed life clashes are necessary parts of lion preservation.

2. **Hostage Settings:**

In hostage conditions, factors like eating routine, dental consideration, and generally speaking wellbeing assume critical parts in keeping a lion's chomp force. Protection endeavors stretch out past the wild, enveloping mindful hostage reproducing programs, veterinary consideration, and public mindfulness drives to guarantee the prosperity of lions in imprisonment.

4.2 Analysis of dental adaptations for hunting and feeding.

Dental transformations in carnivores address an entrancing convergence of structure and capability, finely tuned by the powers of development for the particular difficulties presented by hunting and benefiting from creature prey. This complete examination investigates the assorted cluster of dental transformations saw in carnivores, revealing insight into how these designs have developed to suit different natural specialties, prey inclinations, and hunting procedures.

1. **The Variety of Carnivores: An Environmental Mosaic**
1. **Ordered Variety:**

   Carnivores, having a place with the request Carnivora, incorporate an immense range of animal categories with unmistakable morphologies and biological jobs. This request incorporates notable hunters like enormous felines (Felidae), canids (Canidae), mustelids (Mustelidae), and marine warm blooded animals like seals and ocean lions (Pinnipedia). Every family inside Carnivora displays one of a kind dental transformations molded by its developmental history and environmental specialization.

2. **Environmental Specialties:**

   Carnivores have broadened to involve a great many biological specialties, including earthly, oceanic, and arboreal territories. This variety is reflected in their dietary inclinations, from severe carnivory to omnivory, contingent upon the accessibility of prey and rivalry for assets in their separate surroundings.

   II. General Patterns in Flesh eater Dentition

1. **Carnassial Teeth:**

   One of the trademark dental transformations in carnivores is the presence of carnassial teeth. Carnassials are particular cheek teeth, generally the fourth upper premolar and the main lower molar, intended for shearing and cutting through tissue. This transformation is especially conspicuous in the Felidae family, including lions, tigers, and homegrown felines, as well as in canids like wolves and foxes.

2. **Scissor-Like Activity:**

The plan of carnassial teeth makes a scissor-like activity during jaw development, upgrading the proficiency of slicing through meat and ligaments. This transformation is a demonstration of the specific tensions leaning toward compelling prey handling in rapacious heredities.

III. Felidae: Specific Savage Transformations

1. **Dental Equation:**
The Felidae family, normally known as felines, displays surprising dental transformations customized for carnivory. The dental equation regularly incorporates incisors, canines, premolars, and molars. The number and morphology of these teeth change across species, reflecting transformations to various hunting and taking care of techniques.

2. **Lengthened Canines:**
The canines in felids are lengthened, sharp, and pointed, serving various capabilities in hunting and taking care of. These teeth are critical for conveying a deadly chomp to the neck or throat of prey, helping with both repressing and killing. The size of the canines frequently connects with the size of the prey species a feline normally chases.

3. **Diminished Dentition:**

Felids by and large show a diminished number of teeth contrasted with a few different carnivores. This decrease is a consequence of developmental compromises, as a smoothed out dentition limits weight and works with more quick jaw development during the pursuit and catch of prey.

IV. Canidae: Flexible Trackers with Flexibility

1. **Dental Equation and General Attributes:**
The Canidae family, involving canids like wolves, foxes, and homegrown canines, shows dental transformations that line up with their flexible hunting techniques and omnivorous inclinations. The dental recipe incorporates incisors, canines, premolars, and molars, giving a flexible tool compartment to various dietary things.

2. **Summed up Dentition:**
Canids have a more summed up dentition contrasted with the particular transformations found in certain felids. Their teeth are adjusted for

catching and handling a different scope of prey, including little warm blooded creatures, birds, and at times, rummaging on carcass.

3. **Smashing Molars:**

While canids need carnassial teeth, their molars are adjusted for pounding and crushing. This dental morphology empowers them to handle an assortment of food things, including bones and plant material, upgrading their versatility to changing ecological circumstances and food accessibility.

V. Mustelidae: Versatile Oceanic and Earthbound Hunters

1. **Semiaquatic Transformations:**
The Mustelidae family, enveloping otters, weasels, and badgers, grandstands a scope of dental transformations appropriate for both earthly and semiaquatic ways of life. Their dentition mirrors the different prey things experienced in oceanic conditions, like fish and creatures of land and water, as well as earthbound prey like rodents.

2. **Sharp Canines and Shearing Teeth:**

Mustelids normally have sharp, lengthened canines for seizing and stifling prey. A few animal varieties, similar to the otter, have particular shearing teeth for controlling and consuming fish, stressing the flexibility of their dentition to shifted environmental specialties.

VI. Pinnipedia: Sea-going Specializations for Marine Carnivores

1. **Flippers and Sea-going Ways of life:**
The Pinnipedia family, containing seals, ocean lions, and walruses, has developed to flourish in amphibian conditions. Their dentition is adjusted for hunting and consuming marine prey, like fish and cephalopods. Pinnipeds are described by particular variations in both their appendages and dentition, considering proficient swimming and prey catch.

2. **Decreased and Homodont Dentition:**

Numerous pinnipeds display a decrease in the quantity of teeth and homodonty, where the teeth are comparative in shape. This dental rearrangements lines up with the smoothed out body plan fundamental for quick submerged development. The teeth are adjusted for getting a handle on elusive prey, and at times, for pulverizing shells or destroying bigger fish.

VII. Developmental Drivers: Dietary Specialization and Biological Setting

1. **Coevolution with Prey:**
Flesh eater dentition has advanced pair with the prey species accessible in their particular surroundings. This coevolutionary dynamic is obvious in the specialization of dental elements that upgrade a carnivore's capacity to catch, kill, and cycle explicit prey types. For instance, felids coevolve with herbivores, while canids may coevolve with more modest warm blooded animals and rummaging valuable open doors.
2. **Dietary Versatility:**

Carnivores frequently display dietary pliancy, permitting them to change their taking care of propensities in view of environmental circumstances and prey accessibility. This flexibility is reflected in the flexibility of their dentition, empowering carnivores to take advantage of a scope of food assets and effectively possess different specialties.

VIII. Dental Wear and Upkeep: Signs of Taking care of Propensities

1. **Wear Examples:**
Dental wear designs give significant experiences into the taking care of propensities and biology of carnivores. For example, the presence of wear features on carnivore teeth can show the sorts of prey consumed and the powers applied during gnawing and biting. Wear on the carnassial teeth of felids might uncover the degree of carnivory in their eating regimen.
2. **Dental Upkeep:**

Dental wellbeing is critical for the endurance and regenerative outcome of carnivores. Regular ways of behaving, for example, biting on bones, prepping, and hunting add to dental support. Dental pathologies, including breaks and diseases, can influence a flesh eater's capacity to chase and consume prey, featuring the interconnectedness of dental wellbeing and biological wellness.

IX. Preservation Suggestions: Dentition as a Mark of Biological system Wellbeing

1. **Environment Wellbeing Markers:**
The investigation of meat eater dentition stretches out past grasping their science; it fills in as an important device for checking environment wellbeing. Changes in dentition, like dental anomalies or unreasonable wear, may show shifts in prey populaces, natural surroundings debasement, or the presence of poisons influencing the general soundness of carnivore populaces.
2. **Protection Methodologies:**

Protection endeavors pointed toward saving carnivore populaces should consider the biological variables affecting their dentition. Territory safeguarding, practical administration of prey species, and moderating human-untamed life clashes are indispensable parts of flesh eater preservation. Understanding the dental variations of carnivores adds to informed protection procedures that address the complicated transaction between these hunters, their prey, and their biological systems.

4.3 Implications for survival and ecological niche.

The perplexing snare of life in environments depends vigorously on the variations and associations of species inside their biological specialties. Carnivores, as dominant hunters, assume a vital part in molding the elements of environments. This investigation dives into the ramifications for endurance and biological specialty that emerge from the exceptional qualities and ways of behaving of carnivores. From hunting procedures to natural surroundings inclinations, the exchange between these hunters and their surroundings impacts their endurance as well as the wellbeing and equilibrium of whole environments.

1. **Step by step processes for surviving: Adjusting to Flourish**
1. **Hunting Procedures:**
   Carnivores have developed a different cluster of hunting techniques, finely tuned to their biological jobs and the accessibility of prey in their living spaces. The determination of hunting techniques is many times affected by the size and conduct of prey species, as well as the particular variations of the actual carnivores.

   Pursuit Hunters: A few carnivores, similar to cheetahs, are worked for speed and succeed as pursuit hunters. Their slim bodies, strong appendages, and sharp vision empower them to pursue down prey in open scenes. This technique is successful in conditions where perceivability is high, and the prey's getaway courses are restricted.

   Snare Hunters: Others, like lions and tigers, are proficient trap hunters. They depend on covertness and camouflage to draw near to their prey prior to sending off an unexpected, strong assault. This procedure is powerful in territories with changed geography, offering cover for following and ambushing.

   Pack Hunting: Wolves and African wild canines utilize pack hunting, utilizing social collaboration to build their odds of coming out on top. This procedure is favorable for handling bigger prey and is much of the time found in species that possess different scenes with shifted prey accessibility.

2. **Dietary Specialization:**

Carnivores show fluctuating levels of dietary specialization, impacting their biological jobs and methods for surviving. The dentition and taking care of transformations of carnivores are frequently customized to their favored prey things, mirroring the developmental tensions that have molded their specialties.

Hyper-Carnivores: Species that depend intensely on creature tissue, like large felines, are named hyper-carnivores. Their dentition is adjusted for catching, killing, and handling meat proficiently. These carnivores frequently have particular highlights like extended canines and carnassial teeth for tearing and shearing.

Omnivores: A few carnivores, similar to bears, are crafty omnivores. Their eating regimen incorporates a blend of creature matter and plant material. This dietary adaptability permits them to take advantage of an extensive variety of food assets, adding to their versatility in evolving conditions.

II. Environmental Specialties: The Job in Biological system Elements

1. **Dominant hunters:**

   Carnivores, particularly dominant hunters, stand firm on a remarkable foothold in environments. As top-level hunters, they apply hierarchical control on prey populaces, affecting the overflow and dissemination of species lower in the well established pecking order. This hierarchical guideline is basic for keeping up with biological equilibrium and forestalling overgrazing or uncontrolled multiplication of herbivores.

2. **Trophic Fountains:**

   The presence or nonattendance of carnivores can set off trophic fountains, impacting the design and working of whole environments. Trophic fountains happen when changes in the overflow or conduct of hunters bring about flowing impacts all through the food web. For instance, the renewed introduction of wolves in Yellowstone Public Park prompted a trophic outpouring, with impacts on vegetation, prey species, and, surprisingly, the actual geology of the scene.

3. **Cornerstone Species:**

   Carnivores frequently capability as cornerstone species, assuming a lopsidedly persuasive part in keeping up with biodiversity and environment wellbeing. The expulsion of a cornerstone animal groups can have broad outcomes, prompting shifts in local area construction and environment elements. Wolves, for example, are viewed as cornerstone species in specific environments because of their impact on herbivore populaces and vegetation.

   III. Coevolutionary Elements: Variations In light of Prey

1. **Developmental Weapons contest:**
   Carnivores and their prey take part in an unending developmental weapons contest, with every transformation in one animal varieties driving counter-variations in the other. This coevolutionary dance shapes the natural collaborations among hunters and prey and adds to the adjusting of step by step processes for surviving on the two sides.
   Cover and Guarded Variations: Prey species frequently advance disguise or cautious transformations to avoid hunters. Accordingly, carnivores foster methodologies for further developed identification, like sharp faculties or specific hunting strategies, prompting a ceaseless pattern of variations and counter-transformations.
   Speed and Pursuit: The advancement of speed in prey species is met with the improvement of upgraded pursuit techniques in carnivores. This powerful cooperation impacts the actual characteristics and conduct transformations of the two hunters and prey.
2. **Developmental Compromises:**

   Carnivores face developmental compromises as they adjust to the difficulties of hunting and endurance. Compromises might include energy designation, physical elements, or conduct procedures that improve one part of endurance to the detriment of another. For instance, the energy used in quest for prey should be adjusted against the energy acquired from a fruitful kill.
   IV. Human-Carnivore Connections: Difficulties and Protection Suggestions

1. **Living space Infringement and Discontinuity:**
   Human exercises, like urbanization and rural extension, frequently lead to environment infringement and discontinuity. This brings people and carnivores into closer nearness, prompting expanded possibilities of contention. The deficiency of regular natural surroundings can upset environmental specialties and relocation courses for carnivores, affecting their capacity to get prey and keep up with solid populaces.
2. **Preservation Techniques:**

   Preservation endeavors for carnivores require an extensive comprehension of their environmental specialties and endurance needs. Territory safeguarding, safeguarded regions, and halls for untamed life development are fundamental parts of carnivore protection. Furthermore, methodologies to moderate human-carnivore clashes, for example, secure animals practices and local area based preservation drives, add to the concurrence of people and carnivores.

Chapter 5

Communication Through Cranial Features

Correspondence is a crucial part of the set of all animals, filling different needs like mate fascination, regional flagging, cautioning of risk, and coordination inside gatherings. While vocalizations, non-verbal communication, and compound prompts assume essential parts in creature correspondence, this extensive investigation centers around the frequently disregarded yet similarly huge perspective - correspondence through cranial elements. From prongs and horns to looks and skull morphology, creatures have advanced a variety of cranial transformations that pass on data fundamental for their endurance and social connections. This assessment dives into the captivating universe of cranial correspondence, unwinding the complicated manners by which creatures use their cranial highlights to pass on messages and explore their biological specialties.

1. **Tusks and Horns: Weapons, Signs, and Status**
1. **Horns in Cervids:**
   Horns, noticeable cranial designs tracked down in individuals from the deer family (Cervidae), serve multi-layered jobs in correspondence. Basically borne by guys, tusks are a striking illustration of physically dimorphic cranial highlights that assume a significant part in mate choice and rivalry.

   Mate Fascination: During the mating season, or groove, male deer utilize their horns in showcases to draw in females. The size, evenness, and by and large strength of horns act as signs of hereditary wellness, impacting the mate selection of females.

   Intraspecific Contest: Horns are impressive weapons utilized in intraspecific rivalry among guys. Ritualized battle, including conflicts and shows, decides strength and admittance to mating open doors. The sound delivered during tusk conflicts likewise fills in as a hear-able sign, scaring rivals and declaring predominance.

   Social Pecking order: The size and intricacy of tusks frequently relate with social progressive system inside deer populaces. Prevailing guys with bigger tusks normally appreciate particular admittance to assets, including food and mating accomplices.

2. **Horns in Bovids:**

Horns, tracked down in individuals from the Bovidae family, including sheep, goats, and cows, are one more illustration of cranial highlights essential to correspondence. Dissimilar to prongs, horns are long-lasting designs and are in many cases present in the two guys and females.

Intraspecific Showcases: Horns assume a pivotal part in intraspecific correspondence, particularly during the reproducing season. Male bighorn sheep, for instance, take part in head-butting challenges to lay out predominance and admittance to mating open doors.

Visual Signs: The size, shape, and curve of horns pass on data about a singular's age, wellbeing, and hereditary wellness. In certain species, for example, the African impala, horn length is connected to progress in years and fills in as a visual sign for expected mates.

Safeguard Instruments: Horns likewise capability as guarded weapons against hunters. Bovids utilize their horns to avoid hunters, safeguarding themselves and their posterity. The size and sharpness of horns are critical variables in deflecting expected dangers.

II. Looks: Feelings and Social Elements

1. **Canine Correspondence:**
   In homegrown canines (Canis lupus familiaris) and numerous wild canids, looks are imperative for correspondence inside gatherings and with people. Canines, specifically, have developed a large number of looks that convey feelings and expectations.

   Eyes and Eyebrows: The development and position of a canine's eyebrows, particularly the inward temple raiser muscle, known as the AU101, can convey feelings like shock, trouble, or consideration. Moreover, the size of a canine's students can show fervor, dread, or unwinding.

   Mouth and Lips: The place of a canine's mouth and lips can convey different feelings. A casual, open mouth might demonstrate happiness, while exposed teeth might flag hostility. Lip licking and yawning are frequently utilized as conciliation signals in friendly communications.

   Ear Developments: Canine ears are exceptionally versatile and can move freely. Erect ears might flag sharpness or energy, while leveled ears can demonstrate dread or accommodation.

   Tail developments and body act supplement looks to pass on a more complete message.

2. **Primate Facial Correspondence:**

Looks assume a critical part in primate correspondence, filling in as a rich and nuanced method for communicating feelings and keeping up with social securities.

Mimicry and Signals: Primates, particularly extraordinary chimps, participate in facial mimicry and motions to convey feelings and expectations. Chuckling, for instance, is a social conduct in extraordinary gorillas, including chimpanzees and bonobos, meaning perkiness and holding.

Predominance and Accommodation: Looks are essential to laying out and keeping up with social ordered progressions among primates. Predominant people might show emphatic looks, while agreeable people might show mollification signals, for example, uncovered teeth to flag peace.

Acknowledgment and Association: Primates utilize facial highlights for individual acknowledgment inside their gatherings. This acknowledgment is vital for shaping and keeping up with social bonds, with looks filling in for the purpose of certifying affiliative connections.

III. Skull Morphology: Signifiers of Nature and Conduct

1. **Flesh eater Skulls:**
   Skull morphology in carnivores is unpredictably connected to their taking care of ways of behaving, hunting systems, and environmental jobs. Various transformations in the skull permit carnivores to take advantage of assorted prey things and explore different conditions.
   Rapacious Dentition: Carnivores regularly have advanced carnassial teeth, adjusted for shearing and cutting through meat. The size and state of these teeth change in view of dietary inclinations, with hyper-carnivores like felines having extended, sharp carnassials.
   Skull Size and Strength: The size and strength of the skull mirror the favored prey size and hunting methodologies of carnivores. Huge, strong skulls are found in dominant hunters like enormous felines, empowering them to handle and stifle bigger prey. Conversely, more modest skulls might be adjusted for hunting more modest, more nimble prey.
   Cranial Peaks and Projections: A few carnivores, similar to hyenas, show cranial peaks and bulges that act as connection destinations for strong jaw muscles. These transformations are vital for creating the power expected for pulverizing bones and getting to supplement rich marrow.
2. **Herbivore Skulls:**

Herbivores, adjusted for handling plant material, display unmistakable skull includes that work with productive rumination and absorption of sinewy vegetation.

Herbivorous Dentition: Herbivores regularly have specific dentition for crushing plant material. This incorporates advanced molars with complex surfaces for proficient biting and handling of intense plant strands.

Skull Shape and Jaw Design: The state of herbivore skulls fluctuates in light of their taking care of propensities. Nibblers, similar to ponies, frequently have prolonged skulls with front oriented eyes for all encompassing vision. Programs, like giraffes, have particular skulls adjusted for coming to and consuming foliage at various levels.

Peaks and Horns: A few herbivores, similar to ungulates, may have cranial peaks or horns that serve different capabilities. Horns, specifically, can be utilized in intraspecific correspondence, guard against hunters, and laying out strength inside gatherings.

IV. Intraspecific Correspondence: Ceremonies, Shows, and Flagging

1. **Romance Showcases:**
   Intraspecific correspondence through cranial highlights is noticeable during romance ceremonies, where people signal their preparation to mate and lay out friendly bonds.

   Birds and Plumage: Birds frequently take part in intricate romance showcases including cranial highlights, like beautiful plumage, peaks, or wattles. These elements act as visual signs of wellbeing, hereditary wellness, and preparation to raise.

   Deer and Horn Presentations: Male deer take part in complex tusk shows during the trench to draw in mates. The size, evenness, and by and large state of prongs act as marks of a male's conceptive wellness, impacting female mate decision.

   Primate Vocalizations and Signals: In primates, including extraordinary chimps, romance includes a blend of looks, vocalizations, and motions. Cranial highlights, like facial shading or peaks, may change during estrus cycles, filling in as viewable prompts to expected mates.

2. **Agonistic Presentations:**

   Cranial elements are likewise essential in flagging strength, accommodation, and settling clashes inside gatherings.

   Deer Prong Conflicts: Intraspecific rivalry among male deer includes horn conflicts, where people take part in ritualized battle to lay out predominance. The sound created during these conflicts fills in as a hear-able sign, affecting the way of behaving of adversaries.

   Primate Predominance Motions: Strength and accommodation inside primate bunches are much of the time imparted through cranial elements like looks, peak erection, or uncovered teeth. Predominant people might show emphatic motions, while agreeable people take on pacification signals.

Horns and Head-Interrupting Bovids: Bovid species, like bighorn sheep, participate in head-butting challenges to lay out predominance. The effect and strength of head-butting act as visual and material signs, deciding the pecking order inside the gathering.

V. Developmental Importance: Variations for Endurance and Multiplication

1. **Sexual Determination and Mate Decision:**
   Cranial elements frequently assume a focal part in sexual determination, impacting mate decision and regenerative achievement.

   Peacock Tail Plumes: The intricate tail quills of male peafowls, with their unmistakable eye-spots, are an exemplary illustration of sexual determination. Females select mates in view of the size, evenness, and energy of these cranial elements, characteristic of hereditary wellness.

   Elk Horns and Mate Fascination: Male elk with bigger, more even prongs are liked by females during the mating season. Prongs act as visual signs of a male's hereditary quality, impacting the probability of effective mating and multiplication.

   Primate Facial Hue: In certain primates, facial hue changes during estrus cycles, flagging conceptive availability. Male primates utilize these obvious prompts to distinguish females in estrus and go after mating potential open doors.

2. **Ruthless Variations:**

Cranial transformations in hunters are finely tuned for catching and curbing prey, mirroring the particular tensions forced by their environmental jobs.

Meat eating Dentition: The improvement of specific dentition, including sharp canines and carnassial teeth, is a ruthless transformation found in carnivores. These elements are significant for proficient prey catch, killing, and utilization.

Tactile Variations: Hunters frequently have cranial transformations, like advanced feelings of vision, smell, and hearing. These variations help in identifying prey, organizing bunch chases, and exploring their surroundings really.

Cranial Peaks for Show: A few hunters, as large felines, may have cranial peaks or elements that fill show needs. These highlights might be raised during conflicts with rivals or as a feature of danger showcases to threaten contenders or safeguard domains.

VI. Protection Suggestions: Cranial Elements as Signs of Biological system Wellbeing

1. **Checking Populace Elements:**
   Cranial elements can act as signs of the general wellbeing and elements of creature populaces inside biological systems.

   Tusk Size and Populace Wellbeing: The size and state of horns in deer populaces might give experiences into the soundness of people and the general populace. Changes in prong size or evenness could be demonstrative of natural stressors, living space quality, or hereditary elements.

Horn Development and Environment Conditions: Horn development in specific ungulates is impacted by variables, for example, sustenance and environment conditions. Observing horn development can give data about the accessibility of assets, environment examples, and possible effects on herbivore populaces.

Cranial Irregularities as Wellbeing Pointers: Anomalies in cranial elements, like mutations or wounds, might be characteristic of ecological stressors, illness commonness, or human-actuated influences. Observing such irregularities can help with evaluating the general soundness of creature populaces.

2. **Preservation Procedures:**

Understanding the job of cranial elements in correspondence and variation is fundamental for carrying out compelling preservation systems.

Safeguarding Territory Availability: Protection endeavors ought to focus on the conservation of environment network, permitting species to keep up with regular ways of behaving, including correspondence through cranial highlights. Divided living spaces can disturb mating ceremonies, social elements, and intraspecific correspondence.

Moderating Human-Natural life Clashes: Protection drives ought to address human-untamed life clashes that might influence cranial correspondence. For instance, clashes with huge herbivores like elephants might prompt wounds, influencing cranial highlights. Carrying out measures to limit such contentions is significant for both human and natural life prosperity.

Checking Prize Hunting Effect: In species where cranial highlights are focused on for prize hunting, cautious observing and guideline are fundamental to guarantee manageability. Overexploitation of people with beneficial cranial highlights can prompt populace declines and disturb environmental elements.

5.1Investigating the role of cranial anatomy in lion communication.

Lions (Panthera leo), as dominant hunters and social carnivores, depend on a refined arrangement of correspondence for endurance, coordination inside prides, and regenerative achievement. Among the different features of lion correspondence, the job of cranial life systems, including looks, vocalizations, and primary transformations, stands apart as a vital area of examination. This investigation plans to unwind the unpredictable manners by which cranial elements add to the correspondence elements of lions, revealing insight into the transformative importance and protection ramifications of these variations.

1. Looks: Quiet Prompts in Lion Correspondence

Looks assume a critical part in lion correspondence, with bristle spot designs being unmistakable identifiers. These one of a kind examples act as a type of visual correspondence inside prides. Examining the job of hair spot designs includes understanding how lions use these facial markings for individual acknowledgment and passing on data about age and hereditary wellness.

Stubble spot designs contribute essentially to individual acknowledgment inside a pride, permitting lions to recognize each other. This is fundamental for keeping up with social securities, organizing bunch exercises, and working with helpful ways of behaving like hunting. Furthermore, changes in stubble spot designs over a singular's life expectancy might pass on data about age and hereditary wellness. Lions probably utilize these viewable prompts to survey the experience and conceptive capability of pride individuals, impacting social elements and mate determination.

Facial muscles additionally assume an essential part in lion correspondence, especially during ways of behaving like the flehmen reaction and facial danger shows. The flehmen reaction, including a twisting back of the lips, works with the exchange of pheromones to the vomeronasal organ, adding to synthetic correspondence. Snarling, joined by facial danger shows, fills in as a powerful specialized device, demonstrating predominance, hostility, or cautioning signs to other pride individuals or possible dangers.

2. Vocalizations: The Reverberation of Lion Correspondence

Vocalizations, including thunders, snorts, and contact calls, comprise a critical piece of lion correspondence. Thundering, specifically, fills various needs, including regional correspondence and mate fascination. Examining the job of thundering includes understanding how acoustic properties pass on data about regional limits and conceptive availability.

Thundering is an amazing asset for lions to lay out and shield regional limits. The examination concerning the acoustic properties of thunders can give bits of knowledge into how lions convey data about the size and strength of their pride, deterring rival prides or people from infringing an on their area. Furthermore, varieties in the force and recurrence of thunders during the mating season assume a urgent part in mate fascination, with lions utilizing these vocalizations to flag conceptive preparation and draw in likely mates.

Past thunders, lions participate in various vocalizations, including snorts and contact calls, adding to intra-pride correspondence. Snorts and contact calls work with social holding inside the pride, assisting lions with keeping in touch during exercises like hunting or resting. These vocalizations likewise assume a part in organizing developments during chases, adding to the effectiveness of gathering exercises.

3. Skull Morphology: The Quiet Engineering of Lion Correspondence

The skull morphology of lions is complicatedly connected to their hunting procedures, taking care of ways of behaving, and social motioning inside prides.

Researching cranial variations includes understanding how the construction of the skull works with compelling prey catch, utilization, and correspondence of social progressive system.

Lions' skulls are adjusted for strong jaw muscles, empowering an intense chomp vital for quelling prey. The presence of carnassial teeth, particular for shearing through tissue and ligaments, is a huge cranial variation. Researching the biomechanics of these variations gives bits of knowledge into how lions effectively process prey during taking care of.

A few lions show cranial peaks, tufts of hair on the head, which might assume a part in friendly motioning inside the pride. Conspicuous cranial peaks might flag social strength, impacting communications inside the pride. Researching these elements adds to how we might interpret the elements of social designs inside lion prides and how visual flagging guides in correspondence.

4. Developmental Importance: Adjusting to Convey

The examination concerning the job of cranial life systems in lion correspondence reveals the versatile procedures that have developed after some time, forming the remarkable correspondence collection of these huge felines. Agreeable hunting and living in gatherings are essential for lions' natural potential benefits and have developed to work with correspondence.

Composed hunting, worked with by vocal and visual correspondence, improves the proficiency of prey catch, adding to the endurance of the pride. Lions' capacity to convey regional limits and conceptive status through vocalizations has developmental importance, guaranteeing the regenerative progress of people and the determination of prides.

5. Preservation Suggestions: Understanding for Viable Administration

Figuring out lion correspondence, especially through cranial life systems, holds vital ramifications for lion preservation. Researching how lions express pressure or distress through looks and vocalizations supports distinguishing early marks of expected struggle with people. This data assists progressives with carrying out measures that lessen stressors and advance concurrence among lions and nearby networks.

Facial markings, including bristle spot designs, give a painless strategy to checking individual lions, assessing populace measures, and carrying out designated protection methodologies. Protection hereditary qualities can profit from examinations concerning facial markings, adding to endeavors to safeguard hereditary variety and guarantee the drawn out feasibility of lion populaces.

5.2 Vocalization mechanisms and their connection to cranial structures.

Correspondence through vocalizations is an all inclusive part of the animals of the world collectively, filling different needs, for example, laying an out area, drawing in mates, advance notice of risk, and organizing social ways of behaving. The complicated connection between vocalization instruments and cranial designs is an entrancing area of study that reveals insight into the developmental transformations and biological jobs of various species. In this investigation, we dig into the systems basic creature vocalizations and how these are interconnected with cranial designs, featuring the assorted manners by which creatures have developed to deliver and decipher sounds.

1. **The Premise of Creature Vocalizations: Life systems and Physiology**
1. **Respiratory Framework:**

   The creation of vocalizations in creatures starts with the respiratory framework. In well evolved creatures, including many expressing species, the lungs give the air supply important to sound creation. The stomach and other respiratory muscles control the wind stream, impacting the pitch, volume, and span of vocalizations.

2. **Larynx and Vocal Folds:**

   The larynx, frequently alluded to as the voice box, is a vital part in many creatures' vocalization components. Inside the larynx, vocal folds, otherwise called vocal ropes, assume an essential part. The vibration of these folds, brought about by the section of air, produces sound. The strain and length of the vocal folds decide the pitch, while the power of air and the opening and shutting of the glottis control the volume and force.

3. **Adjusting Reverberation:**

Creatures can additionally adjust the reverberation of vocalizations by changing the shape and size of their vocal parcel. This is accomplished through changes in the place of the tongue, delicate sense of taste, and different designs inside the oral and nasal depressions. The resounding chambers intensify and shape the fundamental sound created by the vocal folds, adding to the uniqueness of various vocalizations.

II. Cranial Designs and Their Impact on Vocalization

1. **Cranial Morphology and Sound Creation:**

   The life structures of the skull assumes a huge part in molding the sounds created by expressing creatures. The size and design of the skull, especially the oral and nasal holes, influence the reverberation and tone of vocalizations. Creatures with specific cranial variations might deliver one of a kind sounds custom-made to their natural requirements.

2. **Skull Size and Reverberation:**

   Creatures with bigger skulls frequently have bigger vocal lots, impacting the full frequencies of their vocalizations. For instance, bigger skulls in specific bird species are related with lower-recurrence calls. Understanding the connection between skull size and reverberation gives experiences into the acoustic systems creatures utilize to impart really inside their surroundings.

3. **Peaks and Projections:**

A few animal groups display cranial peaks, horns, or different bulges that impact the projection and gathering of vocalizations. In ungulates like deer and eland, cranial designs might go about as reverberation chambers, enhancing calls during the mating season. Exploring the acoustic properties of these designs upgrades how we might interpret their job in intraspecific correspondence.

III. Species-explicit Vocalization Transformations

1. **Birds:**

   Syrinx and Tune Intricacy:

   In birds, vocalizations are essentially created by the syrinx, an extraordinary vocal organ situated at the foundation of the windpipe. Birds have developed complex syringeal muscles that take into consideration wonderful command over sound creation. The variety of bird melodies is frequently connected to the intricacy and adaptability of the syrinx. Species-explicit transformations in syringeal structure add to the huge range of bird vocalizations, from resonant melodies to complex calls.

   Cranial Transformations in Woodpeckers:

   Woodpeckers, known for their drumming sounds, have particular cranial transformations that safeguard their cerebrums from the effect powers of quick pecking. Exploring the association between these transformations and vocalization gives bits of knowledge into how woodpeckers use sound for correspondence and scrounging.

2. **Cetaceans:**

   Echolocation in Dolphins and Whales:

   Cetaceans, like dolphins and whales, have advanced modern vocalization systems, including echolocation. The melon, a greasy design in the heads of toothed whales, assumes a critical part in centering and coordinating echolocation clicks. Understanding the cranial designs engaged with echolocation upgrades our enthusiasm for how these marine well evolved creatures explore their surroundings and find prey.

   Social Correspondence in Whales:

   Whales, known for their mind boggling melodies, may have specific cranial variations that impact the creation and gathering of these vocalizations. Researching the acoustic properties of baleen plates, present in some whale species, adds to how we might interpret how these designs might assume a part in friendly correspondence.

3. **Well evolved creatures:**

   Cat Thundering and Hyoid Bone:

   Large felines, including lions, are prestigious for their strong thunders. The hyoid bone, a U-molded bone in the throat, adds to the reverberation of these vocalizations.

Researching the size and construction of the hyoid bone corresponding to the cranial life systems of huge felines offers experiences into the mechanics of their notorious thunders.

Primate Vocalizations and Facial Life structures:

Primates, including people, display a great many vocalizations. The association between cranial designs, especially facial life structures, and vocalizations in primates is unpredictable. Examining the job of looks and cranial variations improves how we might interpret how primates use vocalizations for social correspondence, mate fascination, and communicating feelings.

IV. Transformative Meaning of Vocalization and Cranial Variations

1. **Sexual Determination:**

   Vocalizations frequently assume a part in sexual determination, impacting mate decision and conceptive achievement. Creatures with intricate or unmistakable vocalizations might find true success in drawing in mates. Exploring the cranial transformations related with these vocalizations gives experiences into how sexual choice has formed the development of species-explicit correspondence techniques.

2. **Biological Transformations:**

   Vocalizations and cranial variations are frequently intently attached to environmental specialties. Species possessing thick woods might advance particular vocalizations and cranial designs to upgrade correspondence in such conditions. Researching these variations upgrades how we might interpret how creatures have advanced to flourish in unambiguous natural surroundings.

3. **Social Union:**

In species that depend on friendly designs, vocalizations add to social union. Cranial designs that upgrade the projection and gathering of vocalizations might be leaned toward by normal choice, advancing viable correspondence inside gatherings. Researching the transformative meaning of these variations gives an all encompassing perspective on how creatures explore complex social elements.

V. Protection Suggestions: Saving Correspondence Systems

1. **Anthropogenic Effects:**

   Human exercises, including natural surroundings obliteration and commotion contamination, can disturb creature correspondence. Researching what cranial designs and vocalizations are meant for by anthropogenic elements illuminates preservation procedures pointed toward relieving these impacts. Protecting normal soundscapes and limiting unsettling influences add to the prosperity of species dependent on compelling correspondence.

2. **Observing Populaces:**
   Understanding the association among vocalizations and cranial designs helps with painless checking of natural life populaces. Acoustic observing strategies can be utilized to survey the wellbeing and overflow of species in light of their vocalizations. This approach is especially valuable in remote or testing to-get to environments.

3. **Species-explicit Protection:**

Protection endeavors benefit from a nuanced comprehension of how vocalizations and cranial variations shift across species. Fitting protection systems to the particular correspondence needs of various species guarantees the safeguarding of fundamental ways of behaving and biological jobs.

VI. Future Bearings and Interdisciplinary Methodologies

1. **Mechanical Advances:**
   Progresses in innovation, including high-goal imaging procedures and bio-acoustics, empower analysts to investigate the complicated association between vocalization components and cranial designs. Harmless strategies, for example, CT sweeps and 3D recreations, give itemized bits of knowledge into the inner designs related with sound creation.

2. **Interdisciplinary Coordinated effort:**

The investigation of vocalizations and cranial designs benefits from interdisciplinary coordinated effort. Researcher, anatomists, acousticians, and scientistss can join their mastery to disentangle the intricacies of how creatures produce and see sounds. Incorporating information from different disciplines upgrades how we might interpret the transformative and biological settings of correspondence.

5.3 Social implications of communication within prides.

Correspondence inside lion prides is a complex and nuanced part of their social design, assuming a critical part in keeping up with union, planning exercises, and laying out progressive systems. The rich collection of vocalizations, visual signs, and material collaborations shapes the foundation of public activity among lions. In this investigation, we dig into the social ramifications of correspondence inside prides, revealing insight into how these grand enormous felines explore the complexities of their collective presence.

1. **Vocalizations: The Sonic Texture of Social Bonds**

1. **Thundering as Regional Statement:**
   Lion thunders resound across savannahs and meadows, filling in as strong signs of regional limits. The social ramifications of thundering are multi-layered, mirroring the need to impart regional possession, discourage rival prides, and lay

out aural milestones inside their broad environments. Thundering, frequently performed by predominant guys, adds to the general social character of the pride, building up its presence and strength.

2. **Contact Calls for Social Holding:**

Lions take part in different contact calls, going from delicate snorts to milder thunders, to keep up with social bonds inside the pride. These vocalizations are significant for keeping individuals in nearness, particularly during exercises like hunting or resting. Contact calls cultivate a feeling of solidarity and coordination, guaranteeing that singular lions can rapidly find each other in the immense scenes they possess.

II. Visual Signs: Non-verbal Prompts in Friendly Elements

1. **Looks and Non-verbal communication:**
   Lions convey broadly through looks and non-verbal communication, giving inconspicuous yet fundamental signals to social cooperations. Looks, including scowls, flehmen reactions, and different types of eye to eye connection, convey feelings, goals, and various leveled status. Prevailing people might show self-assured looks, while agreeable individuals might embrace settlement signals. Understanding these visual signs is fundamental for deciphering the complex social elements inside the pride.

2. **Tail Developments and Correspondence:**

Lions use tail developments as a type of correspondence, communicating state of mind, hostility, or accommodation. A raised tail might show fervor or readiness, while a flicking or washing tail might flag bothering or eagerness. During bunch exercises, for example, hunting, noticing the coordination of tail developments gives bits of knowledge into the solidarity and participation among pride individuals.

III. Material Associations: Hardening Social Bonds

1. **Prepping and Connection:**
   Prepping is a material way of behaving that fortifies social bonds inside lion prides. Individuals take part in proportional preparing, for cleanliness purposes as well as a showcase of connection and collaboration. This material communication supports the interconnectedness of people inside the pride, encouraging trust and participation fundamental for common living.

2. **Cuddling and Holding:**

Snuggling, head scouring, and different types of actual contact add to holding between pride individuals. These material ways of behaving are in many cases seen between firmly related people or those with solid social ties. Nestling builds up friendly bonds, lays out a feeling of commonality, and improves the general union of the pride.

IV. Social Progressive system: Correspondence as an Instrument for Request

1. **Predominance Showcases:**
   Correspondence inside lion prides is naturally connected to the foundation and support of social ordered progressions. Predominant people utilize different vocalizations, visual signals, and non-verbal communication to declare their strength. Thundering, joined by a sure stance and decisive looks, builds up the order inside the pride. Subordinate people answer with compliant signs, adding to an amicable social request.

2. **Compromise:**

Lions use correspondence as an instrument for settling clashes inside the pride. Agonistic vocalizations, for example, snarling, joined by visual presentations of predominance or accommodation, serve to de-raise conflicts. Understanding the language of compromise is fundamental for forestalling pointless hostility and keeping up with soundness inside the pride.

V. Conceptive Techniques: Facilitated Correspondence for Progress

1. **Mate Fascination and Romance:**
   Correspondence inside prides arrives at its apex during the mating season. Lions participate in unambiguous vocalizations and ways of behaving to flag regenerative preparation and draw in possible mates. Romance customs include a blend of visual signs, vocalizations, and material collaborations, mirroring the complexities of mate determination and match holding inside the pride.

2. **Correspondence During Fledgling Raising:**

The birth and raising of fledglings include broad correspondence inside the pride. Lionesses impart through delicate vocalizations, visual signs, and material associations to facilitate offspring care. Pride individuals team up to secure and sustain the weak whelps, accentuating the public exertion in guaranteeing the endurance of the future.

VI. Suggestions for Pride Elements and Protection

1. **Social Steadiness and Pride Wellbeing:**
   Powerful correspondence is indispensable to the social security of lion prides. Prides major areas of strength for with networks show more elevated levels of participation, effective hunting tries, and by and large wellbeing. Understanding these elements is vital for the protection of lion populaces, as disturbances in friendly designs can have flowing consequences for pride elements and conceptive achievement.

2. **Human-Natural life Struggle Alleviation:**

Examining the social ramifications of lion correspondence helps with conceiving procedures for alleviating human-natural life clashes. Consciousness of the signs that demonstrate pressure, unsettling, or likely clash inside prides permits protectionists and natural life directors to carry out measures that limit aggravations and cultivate concurrence.

Chapter 6

Pathologies And Anomalies

Lions (Panthera leo), as impressive dominant hunters, are not absolved from the difficulties of wellbeing abnormalities and pathologies that influence both hostage and wild populaces. Understanding the scope of medical problems that lions might experience is significant for preservation endeavors, untamed life the board, and the prosperity of people in bondage. In this investigation, we dig into the assorted range of pathologies and oddities saw in lions, revealing insight into the complexities of their wellbeing, likely causes, and suggestions for both hostage and wild populaces.

1. **Dental Pathologies: Exploring Oral Wellbeing Difficulties**
1. **Tooth Rot and Periodontal Illness:**
   Dental pathologies, for example, tooth rot and periodontal illness, are normal hardships in hostage and wild lions. Factors like age, hereditary qualities, and eat less carbs can add to these issues. Researching the pervasiveness of dental issues gives bits of knowledge into the general wellbeing of lion populaces and the possible effect on their capacity to chase and take care of really.
2. **Malocclusion and Dental Anomalies:**

Malocclusion, a misalignment of teeth, and other dental irregularities might happen because of hereditary elements or wounds. These circumstances can influence a lion's capacity to devour food appropriately, prompting healthful lacks. Understanding the commonness and reasons for malocclusion adds to worked on veterinary consideration for both hostage and wild lions.

II. Irresistible Sicknesses: A Steady Danger to Wellbeing

1. **Cat Immunodeficiency Infection (FIV) and Cat Leukemia Infection (FeLV):**
   Lions are helpless to cat immunodeficiency infection (FIV) and cat leukemia infection (FeLV), which can think twice about insusceptible frameworks. Exploring the predominance of these infections and their transmission elements inside

populaces is urgent for creating successful techniques to alleviate the effect of irresistible illnesses on lion wellbeing.

2. **Canine Sickness and Parasitic Diseases:**

Canine sickness, frequently communicated from homegrown canines, represents a critical danger to lions. Parasitic diseases, including inside parasites like roundworms and outer parasites like ticks and bugs, can prompt different medical problems.

Investigating the study of disease transmission of these contaminations helps in concocting preventive measures and dealing with the wellbeing of both hostage and wild lions.

III. Outer muscle Problems: Exploring Locomotor Difficulties

1. **Osteoarthritis and Joint Issues:**
   Outer muscle issues, including osteoarthritis and joint problems, can affect the portability and generally prosperity of lions. These circumstances might emerge from age-related degeneration, wounds, or hereditary inclinations. Examining the commonness and elements adding to outer muscle problems upgrades how we might interpret lion wellbeing and supports the improvement of the board systems.

2. **Bone Sores and Horrendous Wounds:**

Bone sores and horrendous wounds, like breaks, are seen in both hostage and wild lions. These circumstances might result from battles, falls, or different mishaps. Researching the rate and reasons for bone injuries gives experiences into the elements impacting lion conduct and the possible requirement for clinical intercession.

IV. Regenerative Wellbeing: Ripeness Difficulties and Birth Inconsistencies

1. **Barrenness and Regenerative Problems:**
   Lions might encounter ripeness challenges and regenerative problems that influence their capacity to effectively raise. Examining the variables adding to barrenness, like hormonal irregular characteristics or hereditary elements, is essential for overseeing hostage rearing projects and keeping up with sound wild populaces.

2. **Birth Peculiarities and Neonatal Mortality:**

Birth peculiarities, including intrinsic deformities, can happen in lion offspring, prompting expanded neonatal mortality. Exploring the predominance and reasons for birth oddities gives experiences into the hereditary soundness of lion populaces and supports endeavors to work on rearing outcome in bondage.

V. Social Problems: Disentangling the Mental Difficulties

1. **Hostage Related Pressure and Stereotypic Ways of behaving:**
   Lions in imprisonment might show social issues connected with pressure and repression, including stereotypic ways of behaving like pacing or unnecessary preparing. Exploring the reasons for these ways of behaving assists in planning improving conditions that with advancing the psychological prosperity of hostage lions.
2. **Hostility and Social Elements:**

Hostility and disturbances in friendly elements can happen in both hostage and wild lion populaces. Exploring the triggers for animosity and understanding social designs in prides add to the improvement of the board procedures that upgrade the general government assistance of lions.

VI. Neurological Problems: Unwinding the Secrets of the Cerebrum

1. **Epilepsy and Neurodegenerative Circumstances:**
   Lions might encounter neurological problems, including epilepsy and neurodegenerative circumstances. Researching the pervasiveness and reasons for these issues gives bits of knowledge into the neurological wellbeing of lions and supports the advancement of veterinary consideration conventions.
2. **Horrendous Mind Wounds:**

Horrendous mind wounds can result from battles, falls, or different mishaps in both hostage and wild lions. Exploring the results of such wounds and understanding their drawn out impacts add to the advancement of restoration methodologies and the improvement of generally speaking lion government assistance.

VII. Hereditary Abnormalities: Unwinding the Plan of Lions

1. **Inbreeding Wretchedness and Hereditary Variety:**
   Inbreeding wretchedness, coming about because of mating between firmly related people, can prompt diminished wellness and expanded vulnerability to infections. Exploring the hereditary variety inside lion populaces is fundamental for overseeing hostage reproducing programs and guaranteeing the drawn out feasibility of wild populaces.
2. **Albinism and Coat Variety Abnormalities:**

Hereditary oddities, for example, albinism or surprising coat tones, may happen in lion populaces. Researching the hereditary premise of these irregularities gives bits of knowledge into the variety of lion hereditary qualities and their expected ramifications for variation and endurance.

VIII. Ecological Elements: Effect on Wellbeing and Prosperity

1. **Human-Untamed life Struggle and Stress:**
   Lions might confront wellbeing challenges connected with human-natural life struggle, including pressure related messes. Examining the effect of human exercises on lion wellbeing adds to the advancement of preservation techniques that limit stressors and advance conjunction.

2. **Contamination and Ecological Toxins:**

Ecological toxins, like pesticides or weighty metals, can influence the strength of lions, especially in regions where human exercises present impurities. Exploring the pervasiveness of natural poisons and their effect on lion wellbeing is significant for preservation endeavors in both hostage and wild settings.

IX. Protection Suggestions: From Pathologies to Conservation

1. **Sickness The board and Preventive Methodologies:**
   Understanding the scope of pathologies and peculiarities in lions is fundamental for powerful sickness the board and the improvement of preventive techniques. This information upholds the protection of wild populaces and the prosperity of lions in bondage.

2. **Hereditary Protection and Reproducing Projects:**
   Researching hereditary irregularities and inbreeding discouragement adds to the protection of lion hereditary qualities. Executing hereditary administration techniques, for example, controlled reproducing programs, keeps up with solid hostage populaces and supports hereditary variety in nature.

3. **Veterinary Consideration and Recovery:**
   The examination of different wellbeing challenges in lions illuminates veterinary consideration conventions and recovery systems. Hostage offices and natural life administrators can utilize this information to further develop the general prosperity of lions under their consideration.

4. **Human-Untamed life Struggle Relief:**

Understanding the natural variables adding to lion wellbeing challenges helps with creating techniques for alleviating human-untamed life clashes. Preservation drives that address stressors and ecological pollutants add to the concurrence of lions and neighborhood networks.

X. Future Bearings in Lion Wellbeing Exploration: A Call for Interdisciplinary Joint effort

1. **High level Imaging and Indicative Strategies:**
   Headways in imaging methods, for example, X-ray and CT checks, give valuable chances to point by point examinations concerning lion pathologies and

irregularities. These harmless strategies offer a brief look into the inner designs and conditions influencing lion wellbeing.

2. **Genomic Studies and Sub-atomic Science:**

Genomic studies and sub-atomic science strategies empower specialists to dive further into the hereditary premise of ailments in lions. Understanding the atomic systems hidden pathologies illuminates designated intercessions and hereditary protection techniques.

3. **Conduct Exploration and Improvement Projects:**

Social exploration, combined with the improvement of enhancement programs, adds to the comprehension and the board of pressure related messes in hostage lions. Interdisciplinary joint effort between ethologists, veterinarians, and traditionalists improves the viability of such drives.

6.1 Exploration of common cranial pathologies in captive and wild lions.

Lions (Panthera leo), the magnificent dominant hunters of the African savannah, enrapture our creative mind with their lofty presence. Nonetheless, these famous large felines, whether in imprisonment or meandering the wild, are not safe to different wellbeing challenges that can influence their cranial district. This investigation dives into the normal cranial pathologies saw in both hostage and wild lion populaces, revealing insight into the likely causes, ramifications, and the meaning of understanding and dealing with these circumstances for the preservation and government assistance of these heavenly animals.

1. **Dental Pathologies: Exploring Oral Wellbeing Difficulties**
   Tooth Rot and Periodontal Illness:
   Dental pathologies are common in lions, affecting both hostage and crazy people. Tooth rot and periodontal sickness are normal difficulties, with imprisonment frequently introducing remarkable dangers. Eats less carbs lacking regular abrasiveness add to dental issues in hostage lions, while wild partners might confront difficulties in getting to dental consideration. Examining the pervasiveness of tooth rot and periodontal sickness is critical for executing successful dental consideration rehearses in the two settings.

   Malocclusion and Dental Irregularities:
   Malocclusion, described by misalignment of teeth, and other dental anomalies can influence both hostage and wild lions. Hereditary elements or wounds might add to malocclusion, affecting the lion's capacity to appropriately eat food. Understanding the event and reasons for dental anomalies gives significant experiences into the general wellbeing and dietary difficulties looked by lions.

2. **Awful Wounds: Unwinding the Effect on Cranial Designs**
   Skull Breaks and Head Injury:
   Lions, particularly those in the wild, are inclined to awful wounds, for example,

skull breaks and head injury coming about because of regional debates, hunting occurrences, or mishaps. In imprisonment, cooperations between people or experiences with structures inside walled in areas might prompt comparable wounds. Examining the predominance and reasons for horrendous cranial wounds is fundamental for creating methodologies to forestall such episodes and further develop the general prosperity of lions.

Delicate Tissue Wounds and Hematomas:

Delicate tissue wounds, including hematomas, can happen on the head and face of lions because of battles, falls, or different types of injury. Understanding the recurrence and examples of these wounds helps in surveying the effect of social elements or natural variables on the cranial strength of both hostage and wild lions.

3. **Irresistible Infections: Exploring Wellbeing Dangers**

Contagious and Bacterial Diseases:

Bondage and the wild open lions to different irresistible illnesses, including parasitic and bacterial diseases that can influence the cranial locale. In bondage, where lions might be housed around other people, the gamble of illness transmission is uplifted. In the wild, openness to polluted prey or ecological sources can add to contaminations. Exploring the commonness and transmission elements of these diseases helps with carrying out preventive measures and designated treatment conventions.

Parasitic Pervasions:

Parasitic pervasions, both interior and outside, present wellbeing dangers to lions. Inside parasites, like worms, may affect the stomach related framework, prompting healthful inadequacies. Outside parasites, including ticks and bugs, can cause inconvenience and may communicate illnesses. Investigating the event of parasitic pervasions in hostage and wild lions illuminates methodologies for parasite control and in general wellbeing the executives.

4. **Neurological Problems: Disclosing Cranial Difficulties**

Epilepsy and Seizure Problems:

Lions might encounter neurological problems, including epilepsy and seizure issues. These circumstances can essentially affect the cranial district and generally neurological wellbeing. Exploring the commonness and expected reasons for epilepsy in both hostage and wild lions adds to the improvement of veterinary consideration conventions and the board procedures.

Neurodegenerative Circumstances:

Neurodegenerative circumstances, influencing the mind and sensory system, may appear in cranial side effects. These circumstances could affect the lion's way of behaving, coordination, and in general prosperity. Understanding the event and movement of neurodegenerative circumstances gives experiences into the potential difficulties looked by lions in both hostage and wild settings.

5. **Cranial Cancers: Investigating Development Peculiarities**
Osteosarcoma and Delicate Tissue Growths:
Lions might foster cranial growths, including osteosarcoma influencing the bones of the skull and delicate tissue cancers affecting the cranial district. The commonness of cancers in hostage and wild lions expects examination to comprehend the potential hereditary, natural, or age-related factors adding to their turn of events. Recognizing the sorts of cancers and their effect on lion well-being illuminates therapy choices and protection methodologies.
Meningiomas and Cerebrum Growths:
Meningiomas and other cerebrum growths can influence the cranial designs of lions, prompting neurological side effects. Examining the pervasiveness and attributes of these growths improves how we might interpret their effect on lion conduct and mental capabilities. This information is significant for creating indicative devices and treatment plans for impacted people.

6. **Hereditary Oddities: Disentangling the Outline of Lions**
Craniosynostosis and Formative Oddities:
Hereditary peculiarities might prompt craniosynostosis, a condition where the bones of the skull intertwine rashly, influencing the cranial shape and design. Researching the event of formative peculiarities gives bits of knowledge into the hereditary variety and potential difficulties looked by hostage and wild lion populaces.
Hydrocephalus and Cerebral Anomalies:
Hydrocephalus, described by a collection of cerebrospinal liquid in the mind, and other cerebral irregularities might have a hereditary premise. Understanding the commonness and hereditary variables adding to such irregularities illuminates rearing projects in bondage and adds to the preservation of hereditary variety in nature.

7. **Natural Elements: Effect on Cranial Wellbeing and Government assistance**
Lead Harming and Ecological Impurities:
Lions, especially those in the wild, might be presented to natural impurities, for example, lead, which can affect cranial wellbeing. Researching the event of lead harming and other natural elements influencing the cranial district gives experiences into the potential dangers looked by lions in their environments.
Human-Untamed life Struggle and Cranial Pressure:
Human-untamed life struggle can bring about pressure related messes that might appear in cranial side effects. Exploring the effect of human exercises on lion cranial wellbeing adds to preservation endeavors and procedures pointed toward limiting stressors in both hostage and wild conditions.

8. **Protection Suggestions: From Pathologies to Conservation**
Illness The executives and Hereditary Preservation:
Understanding the pervasiveness of cranial pathologies in lions is critical for

illness the executives and hereditary protection endeavors. Protection programs should consider the hereditary variety and strength of lion populaces to guarantee their drawn out suitability.

Veterinary Consideration Conventions:

Examining cranial pathologies advises the improvement regarding veterinary consideration conventions customized to the particular necessities of hostage and wild lions. These conventions assume a crucial part in tending to medical problems and working on by and large government assistance.

Natural life The board Techniques:

Protectionists and untamed life supervisors can use bits of knowledge into cranial pathologies to foster untamed life the board systems that consider the wellbeing challenges looked by lions in their regular living spaces. This incorporates addressing natural variables and human-untamed life struggle to advance the prosperity of wild populaces.

9. **Future Headings in Cranial Wellbeing Exploration: Propelling Information and Care**

High level Imaging Strategies:

Propels in imaging procedures, for example, X-ray and CT examines, give chances to definite examinations concerning cranial pathologies. Painless strategies empower analysts to picture inside designs and conditions influencing lion cranial wellbeing.

Genomic Studies and Accuracy Medication:

Genomic studies and accuracy medication approaches permit scientists to dive into the hereditary premise of cranial pathologies. Understanding the sub-atomic components fundamental these circumstances illuminates designated intercessions and hereditary protection systems.

Conduct Exploration and Advancement Projects:

Conduct research, combined with the advancement of enhancement programs, adds to the comprehension and the board of pressure related messes in hostage lions. Interdisciplinary cooperation between ethologists, veterinarians, and protectionists upgrades the viability of drives pointed toward advancing mental prosperity.

6.2 Impact of environmental factors on cranial health.

Lions (Panthera leo), the magnificent dominant hunters of the African savannah, enrapture our creative mind with their lofty presence. Nonetheless, these famous large felines, whether in imprisonment or meandering the wild, are not safe to different wellbeing challenges that can influence their cranial district. This investigation dives into the normal cranial pathologies saw in both hostage and wild lion populaces, revealing insight into the likely causes, ramifications, and the meaning of understanding and dealing with these circumstances for the preservation and government assistance of these heavenly animals.

1. **Dental Pathologies: Exploring Oral Wellbeing Difficulties**
   Tooth Rot and Periodontal Illness:
   Dental pathologies are common in lions, affecting both hostage and crazy people. Tooth rot and periodontal sickness are normal difficulties, with imprisonment frequently introducing remarkable dangers. Eats less carbs lacking regular abrasiveness add to dental issues in hostage lions, while wild partners might confront difficulties in getting to dental consideration. Examining the pervasiveness of tooth rot and periodontal sickness is critical for executing successful dental consideration rehearses in the two settings.
   Malocclusion and Dental Irregularities:
   Malocclusion, described by misalignment of teeth, and other dental anomalies can influence both hostage and wild lions. Hereditary elements or wounds might add to malocclusion, affecting the lion's capacity to appropriately eat food. Understanding the event and reasons for dental anomalies gives significant experiences into the general wellbeing and dietary difficulties looked by lions.

2. **Awful Wounds: Unwinding the Effect on Cranial Designs**
   Skull Breaks and Head Injury:
   Lions, particularly those in the wild, are inclined to awful wounds, for example, skull breaks and head injury coming about because of regional debates, hunting occurrences, or mishaps. In imprisonment, cooperations between people or experiences with structures inside walled in areas might prompt comparable wounds. Examining the predominance and reasons for horrendous cranial wounds is fundamental for creating methodologies to forestall such episodes and further develop the general prosperity of lions.
   Delicate Tissue Wounds and Hematomas:
   Delicate tissue wounds, including hematomas, can happen on the head and face of lions because of battles, falls, or different types of injury. Understanding the recurrence and examples of these wounds helps in surveying the effect of social elements or natural variables on the cranial strength of both hostage and wild lions.

3. **Irresistible Infections: Exploring Wellbeing Dangers**
   Contagious and Bacterial Diseases:
   Bondage and the wild open lions to different irresistible illnesses, including parasitic and bacterial diseases that can influence the cranial locale. In bondage, where lions might be housed around other people, the gamble of illness transmission is uplifted. In the wild, openness to polluted prey or ecological sources can add to contaminations. Exploring the commonness and transmission elements of these diseases helps with carrying out preventive measures and designated treatment conventions.
   Parasitic Pervasions:
   Parasitic pervasions, both interior and outside, present wellbeing dangers to

lions. Inside parasites, like worms, may affect the stomach related framework, prompting healthful inadequacies. Outside parasites, including ticks and bugs, can cause inconvenience and may communicate illnesses. Investigating the event of parasitic pervasions in hostage and wild lions illuminates methodologies for parasite control and in general wellbeing the executives.

4. **Neurological Problems: Disclosing Cranial Difficulties**
Epilepsy and Seizure Problems:

Lions might encounter neurological problems, including epilepsy and seizure issues. These circumstances can essentially affect the cranial district and generally neurological wellbeing. Exploring the commonness and expected reasons for epilepsy in both hostage and wild lions adds to the improvement of veterinary consideration conventions and the board procedures.

Neurodegenerative Circumstances:

Neurodegenerative circumstances, influencing the mind and sensory system, may appear in cranial side effects. These circumstances could affect the lion's way of behaving, coordination, and in general prosperity. Understanding the event and movement of neurodegenerative circumstances gives experiences into the potential difficulties looked by lions in both hostage and wild settings.

5. **Cranial Cancers: Investigating Development Peculiarities**
Osteosarcoma and Delicate Tissue Growths:

Lions might foster cranial growths, including osteosarcoma influencing the bones of the skull and delicate tissue cancers affecting the cranial district. The commonness of cancers in hostage and wild lions expects examination to comprehend the potential hereditary, natural, or age-related factors adding to their turn of events. Recognizing the sorts of cancers and their effect on lion wellbeing illuminates therapy choices and protection methodologies.

Meningiomas and Cerebrum Growths:

Meningiomas and other cerebrum growths can influence the cranial designs of lions, prompting neurological side effects. Examining the pervasiveness and attributes of these growths improves how we might interpret their effect on lion conduct and mental capabilities. This information is significant for creating indicative devices and treatment plans for impacted people.

6. **Hereditary Oddities: Disentangling the Outline of Lions**
Craniosynostosis and Formative Oddities:

Hereditary peculiarities might prompt craniosynostosis, a condition where the bones of the skull intertwine rashly, influencing the cranial shape and design. Researching the event of formative peculiarities gives bits of knowledge into the hereditary variety and potential difficulties looked by hostage and wild lion populaces.

Hydrocephalus and Cerebral Anomalies:

Hydrocephalus, described by a collection of cerebrospinal liquid in the mind, and other cerebral irregularities might have a hereditary premise. Understanding the commonness and hereditary variables adding to such irregularities illuminates rearing projects in bondage and adds to the preservation of hereditary variety in nature.

7. **Natural Elements: Effect on Cranial Wellbeing and Government assistance**
   Lead Harming and Ecological Impurities:
   Lions, especially those in the wild, might be presented to natural impurities, for example, lead, which can affect cranial wellbeing. Researching the event of lead harming and other natural elements influencing the cranial district gives experiences into the potential dangers looked by lions in their environments.

   Human-Untamed life Struggle and Cranial Pressure:
   Human-untamed life struggle can bring about pressure related messes that might appear in cranial side effects. Exploring the effect of human exercises on lion cranial wellbeing adds to preservation endeavors and procedures pointed toward limiting stressors in both hostage and wild conditions.

8. **Protection Suggestions: From Pathologies to Conservation**
   Illness The executives and Hereditary Preservation:
   Understanding the pervasiveness of cranial pathologies in lions is critical for illness the executives and hereditary protection endeavors. Protection programs should consider the hereditary variety and strength of lion populaces to guarantee their drawn out suitability.

   Veterinary Consideration Conventions:
   Examining cranial pathologies advises the improvement regarding veterinary consideration conventions customized to the particular necessities of hostage and wild lions. These conventions assume a crucial part in tending to medical problems and working on by and large government assistance.

   Natural life The board Techniques:
   Protectionists and untamed life supervisors can use bits of knowledge into cranial pathologies to foster untamed life the board systems that consider the wellbeing challenges looked by lions in their regular living spaces. This incorporates addressing natural variables and human-untamed life struggle to advance the prosperity of wild populaces.

9. **Future Headings in Cranial Wellbeing Exploration: Propelling Information and Care**

   High level Imaging Strategies:
   Propels in imaging procedures, for example, X-ray and CT examines, give chances to definite examinations concerning cranial pathologies. Painless strategies empower analysts to picture inside designs and conditions influencing lion cranial wellbeing.

   Genomic Studies and Accuracy Medication:

Genomic studies and accuracy medication approaches permit scientists to dive into the hereditary premise of cranial pathologies. Understanding the sub-atomic components fundamental these circumstances illuminates designated intercessions and hereditary protection systems.

Conduct Exploration and Advancement Projects:

Conduct research, combined with the advancement of enhancement programs, adds to the comprehension and the board of pressure related messes in hostage lions. Interdisciplinary cooperation between ethologists, veterinarians, and protectionists upgrades the viability of drives pointed toward advancing mental prosperity.

6.3 The role of research in mitigating cranial anomalies in conservation.

Protection drives are fundamental for defending the wellbeing and prosperity of untamed life populaces, including notable species like lions. Inside the more extensive domain of protection, understanding and relieving cranial oddities in lions require devoted research endeavors. This investigation digs into the critical job of examination in tending to cranial peculiarities, adding to the protection of these magnificent large felines.

1. **Grasping the Causes and Pervasiveness of Cranial Abnormalities**

   Research fills in as the establishment for understanding the causes and commonness of cranial irregularities in lion populaces. By leading far reaching concentrates on both hostage and wild lions, researchers can distinguish hereditary, natural, and anthropogenic variables adding to irregularities like malocclusion, craniosynostosis, and formative anomalies. This information is essential for contriving designated preservation methodologies that address the main drivers of cranial difficulties.

2. **Hereditary Exploration and Preservation Reproducing Projects**

   Hereditary exploration assumes a vital part in moderating cranial oddities, particularly those with a genetic premise. Concentrating on the hereditary variety of lion populaces empowers analysts to distinguish people conveying possibly hindering attributes. Protection rearing projects can then be decisively intended to limit the gamble of inbreeding, a typical figure the improvement of cranial oddities. By incorporating hereditary experiences, moderates plan to improve the strength of lion populaces against cranial difficulties.

3. **Creating Wellbeing The executives Conventions**

   Research adds to the improvement of wellbeing the executives conventions customized to the particular cranial requirements of lions. Point by point concentrates on the life structures, physiology, and pathology of lion skulls empower veterinarians and traditionalists to lay out rules for ordinary wellbeing evaluations, dental consideration, and early location of oddities. Proactive wellbeing the executives forestalls the movement of cranial issues and guarantees the general prosperity of individual lions inside preservation programs.

4. **Observing Ecological Variables and Stressors**

   Natural variables, for example, environment corruption and human-untamed life struggle, can add to cranial pressure in lion populaces. Research helps screen these stressors, giving bits of knowledge into their effect on cranial wellbeing. By understanding how natural changes impact the predominance of cranial irregularities, protectionists can execute measures to relieve pressure related messes. This all encompassing methodology incorporates biological examination with cranial wellbeing evaluations, adding to far reaching preservation systems.

5. **Incorporating Conduct Exploration for Mental Prosperity**

   Cranial wellbeing isn't exclusively a physiological thought; it likewise incorporates mental prosperity. Conduct research assumes an imperative part in grasping how stressors, both regular and human-prompted, influence the way of behaving and emotional well-being of lions. By incorporating conduct experiences into protection techniques, scientists mean to establish conditions that advance mental prosperity, decreasing the event and seriousness of stress-related cranial abnormalities.

6. **Protection Schooling and Local area Commitment**

   Research discoveries on cranial inconsistencies add to protection instruction and local area commitment drives. Instructing neighborhood networks about the significance of lion wellbeing cultivates a feeling of stewardship and empowers dependable practices around lion environments. Furthermore, understanding local area elements and viewpoints through research assists in planning preservation systems that with lining up with the requirements and worries of neighborhood populaces, cultivating cooperative endeavors to alleviate cranial difficulties.

7. **Progressing Demonstrative Innovations for Early Intercession**

   Research-driven headways in demonstrative advancements assume an essential part in early mediation for cranial irregularities. Painless strategies, like high level imaging (X-ray and CT checks), empower analysts and veterinarians to distinguish inconsistencies at their beginning phases.

   Early mediation can then incorporate designated clinical medicines, dental strategies, or, in extreme cases, careful intercessions. Research-driven analytic devices add to the general wellbeing and life span of lions inside preservation programs.

8. **Cooperative Interdisciplinary Exploration**

   Relieving cranial peculiarities in protection requires cooperative interdisciplinary exploration. Uniting specialists in natural life science, hereditary qualities, veterinary medication, environment, and humanities makes a synergistic way to deal with understanding and tending to cranial difficulties. Cooperative exploration endeavors improve the viability of protection techniques by considering the complicated interchange of natural, ecological, and human variables.

9. **Protection Methodologies Informed by Exploration Bits of knowledge**
Research experiences straightforwardly advise the turn of events and refinement regarding protection methodologies pointed toward alleviating cranial irregularities in lions. These techniques include natural surroundings reclamation, local area based preservation, hereditary administration, and wellbeing checking programs. By integrating research-driven information into protection rehearses, drives become more versatile, proof based, and receptive to the developing difficulties looked by lion populaces.

10. **Future Headings in Cranial Peculiarity Exploration**

As preservation challenges advance, future examination bearings ought to zero in on creative ways to deal with relieving cranial irregularities in lions. This remembers utilizing headways for genomics, man-made brainpower for demonstrative examination, and long haul environmental observing. Moreover, exploration ought to investigate the more extensive ramifications of cranial wellbeing on populace elements, environment associations, and the supportability of protection endeavors.

Chapter 7

Technological Advances In Cranial Studies

The investigation of cranial designs has gone through a significant change lately, because of uncommon innovative advances. This investigation digs into the bunch manners by which state of the art advancements have reformed cranial examinations. From customary physical examinations to cutting edge imaging procedures and computational investigations, these advancements have developed how we might interpret cranial designs as well as opened new roads for research, clinical applications, and preservation endeavors.

1. **Prologue to Cranial Examinations and Authentic Setting**

   Cranial examinations have for some time been a foundation of physical exploration, following their underlying foundations back to old civic establishments where perceptions were essentially founded on analyzations and imaginative portrayals. As logical techniques advanced, so did the apparatuses for concentrating on the many-sided designs of the skull. The approach of mechanical forward leaps has pushed cranial examinations into another period, working with an extensive investigation of physical subtleties, useful viewpoints, and neurotic circumstances.

2. **High level Imaging Strategies: Uncovering the Secret Aspects**
   Registered Tomography (CT) Filtering:

   One of the critical mechanical progressions in cranial examinations is the boundless utilization of Figured Tomography (CT) checking. This harmless imaging method considers itemized cross-sectional pictures of the skull, uncovering inward designs with extraordinary clearness. With regards to cranial investigations, CT filtering gives bits of knowledge into bone thickness, sinus morphology, and the multifaceted game plans of the cranial vault. The capacity to envision both delicate and hard tissues in three aspects has reformed how we might interpret cranial life structures and pathology.

   Attractive Reverberation Imaging (X-ray):

Attractive Reverberation Imaging (X-ray) is another strong imaging methodology that has changed cranial investigations. Dissimilar to CT examines, X-ray uses attractive fields and radio waves to create itemized pictures of delicate tissues.

In cranial exploration, X-ray is instrumental in concentrating on the cerebrum, meninges, and cranial nerves, giving a far reaching perspective on the mind boggling brain structures. The capacity to separate between different delicate tissues upgrades how we might interpret cranial pathologies, formative abnormalities, and neurological circumstances.

3. **Three-Layered (3D) Imaging and Printing: Making Accuracy from Information**

Three-Layered Reproduction:

The joining of 3D imaging advances has raised cranial investigations higher than ever. Three-layered reproductions, got from CT and X-ray checks, give specialists a virtual model of the skull, considering top to bottom investigations of physical elements. This innovation works with the investigation of complicated connections between various cranial parts, offering a powerful point of view that rises above conventional two-layered portrayals.

3D Imprinting in Cranial Examinations:

The union of 3D imaging and printing innovations has introduced another time of substantial investigation. Analysts can now make an interpretation of virtual 3D reproductions into actual models through 3D printing. This unmistakable portrayal of cranial designs fills different needs, from instructive devices for understudies and clinicians to preoperative anticipating complex surgeries. In cranial examinations, 3D printing has demonstrated significant for physical exploration, clinical preparation, and customized medication.

4. **Computational Displaying and Reproduction: A Virtual Lab**

Limited Component Investigation (FEA):

Computational displaying procedures, especially Limited Component Examination (FEA), have become key in the domain of cranial investigations. FEA empowers specialists to reproduce the mechanical way of behaving of cranial designs under various circumstances, giving experiences into pressure appropriation, load-bearing limits, and reactions to outside powers. This virtual research center methodology has suggestions for understanding biomechanics, developmental transformations, and the effect of cranial peculiarities on underlying honesty.

Liquid Elements and Cerebrospinal Liquid (CSF) Studies:

Computational reenactments reach out past the primary parts of the skull to investigate liquid elements inside the cranial pit. Cerebrospinal liquid (CSF) elements, fundamental for mind wellbeing, can be reenacted utilizing computational models. These reenactments offer experiences into the dissemination designs, pressure angles, and possible ramifications for neurological circumstances.

The mix of liquid elements into cranial examinations upgrades how we might interpret the powerful exchange among construction and capability.

5. **High level Atomic Imaging: Deciphering the Sub-atomic Scene**
Positron Emanation Tomography (PET) and Single Photon Outflow Figured Tomography (SPECT):
Notwithstanding primary imaging, high level sub-atomic imaging procedures add to the extensive investigation of cranial designs. Positron Discharge Tomography (PET) and Single Photon Outflow Figured Tomography (SPECT) use radioactive tracers to picture metabolic and atomic cycles inside the mind. These methods have applications in concentrating on neurodegenerative sicknesses, growth digestion, and practical parts of the cranial locale.

Optical Soundness Tomography (OCT):
For a tiny scope, Optical Intelligence Tomography (OCT) has arisen as an important instrument for cranial investigations. This harmless imaging strategy utilizes light waves to create high-goal, cross-sectional pictures of tissues. In cranial exploration, OCT empowers itemized representation of microstructures inside the skull, supporting the investigation of bone thickness, microvasculature, and the effect of different obsessive circumstances.

6. **Man-made brainpower and AI: Upgrading Investigation**
Mechanized Division and Comment:
The flood of huge measures of imaging information in cranial examinations has led to the utilization of Computerized reasoning (artificial intelligence) and AI (ML) calculations. Computerized division and explanation of cranial designs, like bones, veins, and brain connections, smooth out the investigation interaction. These innovations upgrade the productivity and precision of information translation, permitting scientists to zero in on more profound bits of knowledge as opposed to difficult manual errands.

Analytic Emotionally supportive networks:
Computer based intelligence controlled indicative emotionally supportive networks are changing cranial examinations by offering wise instruments for design acknowledgment and peculiarity identification. In clinical settings, these frameworks help in the early conclusion of cranial pathologies, like cancers or vascular irregularities. By utilizing AI calculations prepared on different datasets, symptomatic emotionally supportive networks add to additional exact and ideal clinical appraisals.

7. **Computer generated Reality (VR) and Increased Reality (AR): Vivid Investigation**
Augmented Reality (VR) for Cranial Investigation:
Computer generated Reality (VR) has arisen as a strong mechanism for vivid

cranial investigation. Analysts and instructors can step into virtual conditions that recreate the complexities of the cranial designs. This innovation upgrades the comprehension of spatial connections, taking into account intuitive growth opportunities. In clinical preparation, VR works with mimicked medical procedures and physical analyzations, offering a powerful way to deal with cranial examinations.

Expanded Reality (AR) in Careful Preparation:

In the domain of careful mediations connected with cranial irregularities, Expanded Reality (AR) has turned into a priceless device. Specialists can utilize AR to overlay virtual pictures onto the ongoing careful field, giving direction to complex strategies. This innovation upgrades accuracy, diminishes chances, and further develops results in cranial medical procedures. From cancer resections to cranial recreations, AR is changing the manner in which specialists approach mediations.

8. **High-Goal Microscopy: Looking into the Microcosm**

   Examining Electron Microscopy (SEM) and Transmission Electron Microscopy (TEM):

   For analysts diving into the minuscule complexities of cranial designs, high-goal microscopy strategies like Examining Electron Microscopy (SEM) and Transmission Electron Microscopy (TEM) offer unrivaled experiences. These techniques empower the representation of cell and subcellular structures, giving a more profound comprehension of the creation and association of tissues inside the skull. From bone microarchitecture to neuronal associations, high-goal microscopy adds to an all encompassing perspective on cranial life structures.

9. **Mechanical technology in Surgeries: Accuracy and Negligibly Obtrusive Methodologies**

   Robot-Helped Cranial Medical procedures:

   The combination of mechanical technology into surgeries has reclassified the scene of cranial mediations. Robot-helped medical procedures offer improved accuracy, adroitness, and the capacity to explore complex physical designs with negligible intrusiveness. From growth evacuations to mind boggling cranial recreations, advanced mechanics innovation is reshaping the field of cranial medical procedure, prompting worked on understanding results and diminished post-operative intricacies.

10. **Constant Useful Imaging: Checking Dynamic Cycles**

    Practical Attractive Reverberation Imaging (fMRI) and Electroencephalography (EEG):

    Ongoing utilitarian imaging methods add to the unique comprehension of cranial designs during different exercises. Utilitarian Attractive Reverberation Imaging (fMRI) permits specialists to notice changes in blood stream and oxygenation, giving experiences into cerebrum action. Electroencephalography

(EEG) records electrical action in the cerebrum, empowering the investigation of brain processes progressively. These advancements have applications in mental examination, nervous system science, and the investigation of cranial reactions to improvements.

11. **Wearable Advances for Cranial Observing: Movability and Long haul Evaluation**

Wearable Sensors and Neuroimaging:

Headways in wearable advancements have stretched out into the domain of cranial examinations. Wearable sensors, including electroencephalogram (EEG) headsets, offer convenientce for persistent checking of cranial exercises. These gadgets give important information to long haul evaluations of neurological circumstances, rest examples, and reactions to natural boosts. The reconciliation of wearable neuroimaging advancements opens roads for certifiable applications in both exploration and clinical diagnostics.

12. **Applications in Human studies, Legal sciences, and Fossil science**

Criminological Cranial Examination:

Mechanical advances in cranial examinations have essentially affected legal science. Measurable specialists use imaging advancements, computational examinations, and 3D reproductions to distinguish people in light of cranial remaining parts. The accuracy managed the cost of by these advances upgrades criminological examinations, adding to the goal of legitimate cases and the foundation of character.

Anthropological Exploration and Virtual Reproductions:

In the area of humanities, mechanical developments have worked with virtual recreations of cranial designs from archeological remaining parts. CT sweeps and 3D imaging permit scientists to carefully remake skulls, giving bits of knowledge into old populaces, movement designs, and developmental transformations. These virtual recreations add to a more profound comprehension of mankind's set of experiences and natural variety.

13. **Protection and Untamed life Studies: Harmless Bits of knowledge**

Painless Observing of Wild Populaces:

In the domain of natural life preservation, mechanical advances in cranial examinations offer harmless techniques for checking wild populaces. Remote imaging strategies, for example, camera traps furnished with facial acknowledgment calculations, empower analysts to concentrate on individual creatures in light of unmistakable cranial highlights. This harmless methodology upgrades protection endeavors by giving significant information on populace elements, wellbeing, and ways of behaving.

Genomic Advancements for Preservation Hereditary qualities:

Mechanical headways stretch out to the genomic level in preservation hereditary qualities. Scientists utilize progressed genomic devices to concentrate on the hereditary variety of wild populaces, including the examination of cranial attributes impacted by hereditary qualities. Understanding the hereditary premise of cranial highlights adds to protection systems pointed toward saving the transformative potential and flexibility of species in their regular natural surroundings.

14. **Moral Contemplations and Future Headings**

Moral Contemplations in Cranial Examinations:

As mechanical capacities keep on growing, moral contemplations in cranial examinations become progressively significant. Issues connected with security, assent, and capable utilization of delicate imaging information should be painstakingly tended to. Guaranteeing that mechanical headways are applied morally is fundamental for keeping up with the trustworthiness of cranial examination and its applications in different fields.

Future Bearings in Cranial Examinations:

The direction of cranial investigations is ready for proceeded with advancement and investigation. Future bearings incorporate the refinement of artificial intelligence calculations for more precise demonstrative help, the coordination of multi-modular imaging for complete appraisals, and progressions in neuroprosthetics and cerebrum PC interfaces. Also, interdisciplinary joint efforts between innovation engineers, clinicians, and specialists will drive the development of cranial investigations into new wildernesses.

7.1Overview of modern techniques in studying lion cranial anatomy.

The investigation of lion cranial life structures has developed essentially throughout the long term, moved by progressions in innovation and logical procedures. Current methods have furnished scientists with exceptional bits of knowledge into the complexities of lion skulls, considering an exhaustive comprehension of their construction, capability, and variations. This outline investigates the key contemporary strategies utilized in concentrating on lion cranial life structures, revealing insight into the groundbreaking effect of these procedures on our insight into these notorious large felines.

1. **Imaging Innovations: Looking Inside the Skull**
   Registered Tomography (CT) Checking:
   Among the first advancements in lion cranial examinations is Processed Tomography (CT) filtering. This harmless imaging procedure uses X-beams to make nitty gritty cross-sectional pictures of the skull. In lion life systems research, CT checking considers exact perception of bone designs, dental highlights, and delicate tissues. The three-layered recreations got from CT checks give specialists a virtual model of the lion skull, empowering inside and out examinations without the requirement for analyzation.

Attractive Reverberation Imaging (X-ray):

Attractive Reverberation Imaging (X-ray) is one more significant device in the investigation of lion cranial life systems. Dissimilar to CT examines, X-ray utilizes attractive fields and radio waves to create high-goal pictures of delicate tissues. In lion research, X-ray is especially valuable for looking at the mind, cranial nerves, and other sensitive designs. The capacity to separate between different delicate tissues upgrades how we might interpret neuroanatomy and adds to the more extensive investigation of lion cranial capability.

Three-Layered (3D) Imaging and Printing:

Headways in imaging advances reach out to the domain of three-layered (3D) imaging and printing. Specialists can make virtual 3D recreations of lion skulls in view of CT and X-ray information, giving a nitty gritty portrayal of cranial designs. Additionally, 3D printing considers the actual propagation of these virtual models, offering unmistakable examples for instructive purposes, similar investigations, and public commitment. This innovation upgrades openness and works with cooperative examination in lion cranial life structures.

2. **Computational Displaying: Reenacting Cranial Elements**

   Limited Component Investigation (FEA):

   Computational demonstrating, especially Limited Component Examination (FEA), assumes a critical part in reproducing the biomechanics of lion cranial designs. FEA empowers scientists to evaluate how the skull answers various powers, giving experiences into angles like chomp mechanics and primary uprightness. By demonstrating anxiety disseminations, FEA adds to how we might interpret versatile elements in lion skulls and how these transformations impact taking care of conduct and biological specialty.

   Liquid Elements Recreations:

   Notwithstanding underlying reproductions, liquid elements demonstrating is utilized to concentrate on the progression of cerebrospinal liquid (CSF) inside the lion skull. This part of computational exploration offers experiences into the elements of CSF course, possibly impacting neurological wellbeing. Understanding liquid elements upgrades our perception of the physiological elements of the lion cranial cavity and its variations to keep up with ideal circumstances for cerebrum capability.

3. **Hereditary and Sub-atomic Investigations: Disentangling the Hereditary Outline**

   Genomic Studies:

   Headways in hereditary examination have opened new roads for concentrating on lion cranial life structures. Genomic studies permit scientists to investigate the hereditary premise of cranial highlights, varieties, and peculiarities inside lion populaces. By examining the lion genome, researchers can recognize qualities related with cranial turn of events, bone thickness, and different attributes. This hereditary point of view adds to how we might interpret the inherited parts of cranial morphology and illuminates more extensive preservation procedures.

Sub-atomic Markers and Formative Pathways:

Sub-atomic markers and formative pathways give experiences into the atomic cycles administering cranial improvement in lions. Scientists can look at the articulation examples of qualities engaged with skull development, offering a sub-atomic diagram of cranial turn of events. Understanding the flagging pathways and administrative instruments impacting lion cranial life structures adds to the more extensive field of transformative formative science (evo-devotional) and features the hereditary underpinnings of morphological variety.

4. **Anthropological Procedures: Applying Human Strategies to Lion Life structures**

Anthropometric Estimations:

Anthropometric estimations, ordinarily utilized in human life structures studies, have tracked down applications in lion cranial examination. These estimations include measuring different elements of the lion skull, like cranial length, width, and facial highlights. Relative examinations with anthropometric information from other huge feline species or authentic lion examples add to how we might interpret size varieties and developmental patterns in lion cranial life structures.

Cranial Morphometrics:

Cranial morphometrics includes the quantitative examination of cranial shape and size. Utilizing tourist spots and mathematical morphometrics, scientists can evaluate unobtrusive varieties in lion cranial morphology. This procedure takes into account the measurable examination of shape contrasts among various lion populaces or among guys and females. Cranial morphometrics upgrades accuracy in portraying morphological variety and helps in distinguishing versatile elements.

5. **Social and Useful Examinations: Incorporating Environment and Life structures**

Taking care of Conduct Perceptions:

Perceptions of lion taking care of conduct give important experiences into the useful parts of cranial life systems. Specialists can associate skull highlights with taking care of methodologies, nibble force elements, and dietary inclinations. For example, concentrating on how lions process prey things and the job of cranial transformations in taking care of productivity adds to how we might interpret the natural specialty involved by these enormous felines.

Practical Morphology Studies:

Practical morphology concentrates on overcome any barrier among life systems and conduct, zeroing in on the connection between physical designs and their useful ramifications. In lion cranial exploration, utilitarian morphology investigates how explicit highlights, like tooth morphology or jaw mechanics, are adjusted to the requests of their biological jobs. Coordinating practical and physical examinations gives a comprehensive perspective on how cranial designs work with different ways of behaving basic to lion endurance.

6. **High level Microscopy: Examining Tiny Designs**
High-Goal Microscopy Methods:
High level microscopy methods, including Filtering Electron Microscopy (SEM) and Transmission Electron Microscopy (TEM), empower specialists to test infinitesimal designs inside lion cranial tissues. These techniques offer nitty gritty perspectives on bone microarchitecture, dental finish, and cell game plans. By investigating the microcosm of lion cranial life systems, scientists gain bits of knowledge into the better subtleties of tissue organization and variations.

7. **Protection Applications: Harmless Checking**
Painless Checking Strategies:
The utilization of current strategies in lion cranial examinations reaches out to preservation endeavors. Harmless checking methods, for example, camera traps and facial acknowledgment programming, permit analysts to follow individual lions in light of particular cranial elements. This non-problematic methodology supports populace checking, wellbeing evaluations, and the execution of designated preservation techniques without direct intercession.

Genomic Protection Systems:
Genomic advancements utilized in lion cranial examinations have direct ramifications for protection hereditary qualities. Understanding the hereditary variety and genetic variables impacting cranial elements helps with creating protection procedures that focus on the safeguarding of versatile characteristics. Genomic bits of knowledge add to the more extensive objective of keeping up with strong and hereditarily different lion populaces in nature.

8. **Moral Contemplations and Future Bearings**

Moral Contemplations in Lion Cranial Examinations:
The combination of present day strategies in lion cranial examinations requires cautious thought of moral ramifications. Moral contemplations envelop the empathetic treatment of creatures in research, capable information the board, and straightforward correspondence in protection endeavors. Offsetting logical request with moral standards guarantees that progressions in lion cranial examinations add to information without compromising the government assistance of these creatures.

Future Bearings in Lion Cranial Examinations:
The eventual fate of lion cranial examinations holds invigorating possibilities for additional development. Headways in imaging advancements, including higher-goal sweeps and continuous imaging modalities, will give significantly more noteworthy clearness in concentrating on lion cranial designs.

Proceeded with interdisciplinary joint effort, consolidating hereditary examinations with conduct perceptions and biological exploration, guarantees a more extensive comprehension of the versatile methodologies encoded in lion cranial life systems.

7.2 Radiographic and imaging methods for detailed analysis.

Radiographic and imaging techniques have become fundamental devices in the definite examination of cranial life systems. These strategies offer specialists, clinicians, and progressives the capacity to painlessly investigate the many-sided structures inside the skull, giving important bits of knowledge into physical highlights, useful transformations, and obsessive circumstances. This conversation investigates key radiographic and imaging techniques utilized for nitty gritty examination in cranial examinations, featuring their importance and applications.

1. **Figured Tomography (CT) Filtering: Revealing Three-Layered Subtleties Rule and Cycle:**

   Registered Tomography (CT) checking, frequently alluded to as Feline filtering, is a strong imaging method that uses X-beams to make cross-sectional pictures of the skull. This painless technique includes the revolution of a X-beam source around the item, catching numerous pictures that are then reproduced into nitty gritty three-layered portrayals. In cranial examinations, CT filtering is especially important for envisioning bone designs, dental elements, and delicate tissues with high spatial goal.

   Applications in Cranial Examinations:

   CT examining gives unrivaled experiences into the interior engineering of the skull. Analysts use CT pictures to analyze cranial morphology, distinguish physical varieties, and study the spatial connections between various designs. This strategy is fundamental for making virtual 3D reproductions, empowering top to bottom examinations of cranial transformations, biomechanics, and obsessive circumstances. Also, CT checks are significant in clinical settings for diagnosing and arranging medicines for cranial issues.

2. **Attractive Reverberation Imaging (X-ray): Looking into Delicate Tissues Rule and Interaction:**

   Attractive Reverberation Imaging (X-ray) is a painless imaging methodology that utilizes solid attractive fields and radio waves to produce definite pictures of delicate tissues inside the skull. Dissimilar to CT filters, which basically feature thick designs like bones, X-ray is especially successful in picturing mind tissues, cranial nerves, and other delicate designs. The method depends on the attractive properties of hydrogen iotas in the body.

   Applications in Cranial Examinations:

   In cranial examinations, X-ray assumes a critical part in looking at brain structures and delicate tissues that are not very much outlined in CT filters. Scientists use X-ray to research cerebrum life systems, concentrate on the circulation of cerebrospinal liquid (CSF), and evaluate the effect of different neurological circumstances on cranial designs. The capacity to separate between various sorts of delicate tissues improves how we might interpret the powerful parts of cranial life structures and pathology.

3. **Three-Layered (3D) Imaging: Upgrading Perception**
   Guideline and Interaction:
   Three-layered (3D) imaging advances upgrade the perception of cranial designs by making spatially exact models. These models are frequently gotten from CT or X-ray information, giving a more exhaustive portrayal of the skull than customary two-layered pictures. Different programming apparatuses work with the control and investigation of 3D recreations.

   Applications in Cranial Examinations:
   The utilizations of 3D imaging in cranial examinations are different. Scientists influence 3D recreations to concentrate on the morphology of explicit cranial highlights, survey physical varieties, and investigate the connections between various parts of the skull. In instructive settings, 3D models upgrade opportunities for growth by giving intelligent representations of complicated cranial designs. Also, 3D printing innovation considers the production of actual models, helping with involved investigation and correspondence of discoveries.

4. **Fluoroscopy: Dynamic Imaging Continuously**
   Standard and Cycle:
   Fluoroscopy is an ongoing imaging strategy that includes the consistent catch of X-beam pictures as a differentiation specialist is brought into the body. This powerful strategy considers the representation of moving designs and ongoing changes inside the cranial district. Fluoroscopy is especially helpful for concentrating on powerful cycles, like the progression of difference through veins.

   Applications in Cranial Examinations:
   While less normally utilized in static cranial life systems studies, fluoroscopy tracks down applications in the unique evaluation of specific circumstances. For instance, specialists might utilize fluoroscopy to concentrate on the movement and usefulness of the temporomandibular joint (TMJ) during exercises like biting. This continuous imaging ability gives experiences into the biomechanics of cranial designs.

5. **Cone Shaft Registered Tomography (CBCT): Particular Imaging**
   Rule and Interaction:
   Cone Pillar Processed Tomography (CBCT) is a particular type of CT checking that utilizes a cone-molded X-beam shaft for imaging. This strategy is especially appropriate for high-goal checks with lower radiation portions, making it profitable for explicit cranial applications. CBCT is regularly utilized in dental and maxillofacial imaging.

   Applications in Cranial Examinations:

CBCT has tracked down applications in dental and craniofacial studies, giving nitty gritty pictures of the jaw, teeth, and encompassing designs. Specialists and clinicians use CBCT to survey dental life structures, distinguish dental pathologies, and plan intercessions like dental inserts. The engaged idea of CBCT examines makes them significant for restricted examinations inside the cranial locale.

6. **Positron Outflow Tomography (PET) and Single Photon Emanation Processed Tomography (SPECT): Sub-atomic Imaging**

Rule and Interaction:

Positron Outflow Tomography (PET) and Single Photon Emanation Processed Tomography (SPECT) are sub-atomic imaging methods that include the infusion of radioactive tracers. These tracers transmit positrons or gamma beams, taking into consideration the discovery of metabolic and sub-atomic cycles inside the body. While PET uses positron-transmitting tracers, SPECT depends on gamma-radiating tracers.

Applications in Cranial Examinations:

In cranial examinations, PET and SPECT add to the investigation of utilitarian angles at the sub-atomic level. These procedures are utilized to concentrate on cerebral digestion, identify anomalies in synapse frameworks, and evaluate conditions like growths or neurodegenerative issues. Sub-atomic imaging gives a correlative layer of data to primary imaging modalities like CT and X-ray.

7.3Contributions to broader fields, including paleontology and veterinary science.

The bits of knowledge acquired from cranial investigations reach out past the limits of unadulterated life structures, making huge commitments to different fields like fossil science and veterinary science. The information got from the assessment of cranial designs, variations, and pathologies not just develops how we might interpret the developmental past yet additionally illuminates contemporary veterinary practices. This conversation investigates the critical commitments of cranial examinations to more extensive logical areas.

1. **Fossil science: Opening Transformative Accounts**

   Cranial examinations assume a pivotal part in unwinding the transformative history of species, contributing considerably to the area of fossil science. Fossils, especially skulls and cranial remaining parts, act as fundamental hints to reproducing the morphological variations and transformative directions of wiped out organic entities. Through careful examination of cranial designs, scientistss can recognize key elements connected with taking care of ways of behaving, natural specialties, and the general life systems of old animals.

   The assessment of fossilized skulls permits researchers to follow the advancement of different species throughout land time scales. Morphological changes in cranial designs can show variations to ecological movements, changes in dietary inclinations, and even give bits of knowledge into the development of new species. By looking at the cranial life systems of wiped out creatures with those of contemporary species, scientistss can build developmental stories and gain a more profound comprehension of the elements that significantly influenced life on The planet.

2. **Veterinary Science: Propelling Analysis and Treatment**

Cranial examinations have critical ramifications for veterinary science, affecting the conclusion, treatment, and generally speaking consideration of creatures in assorted settings. Veterinary experts influence bits of knowledge from cranial life systems to address an assortment of wellbeing concerns, going from dental issues to neurological circumstances. Understanding the subtleties of cranial designs in various creature species is urgent for giving compelling veterinary consideration.

Dental Wellbeing and Oral Medical procedure:

In veterinary dentistry, the investigation of cranial life systems is basic for diagnosing dental issues and carrying out oral procedures. Information on tooth structure, jaw mechanics, and the arrangement of cranial bones is fundamental for resolving issues like malocclusions, dental breaks, and periodontal infections. Veterinary dental specialists apply standards got from cranial examinations to carry out exact dental methods and work on the general oral soundness of creatures.

Neurological Issues:

Cranial examinations contribute fundamentally to the comprehension of neurological problems in creatures. Conditions influencing the cerebrum, cranial nerves, or spinal line frequently manifest in unambiguous changes in cranial designs. High level imaging strategies, including CT and X-ray filters, permit veterinarians to painlessly analyze the cranial district and analyze issues like growths, awful wounds, or innate oddities. This information guides treatment plans and careful mediations for creatures with neurological issues.

Muscular Contemplations:

In muscular veterinary medication, cranial examinations are applicable to figuring out the construction and capability of joints and bones. Conditions influencing the cranial part of joints, for example, the temporomandibular joint (TMJ) in the skull, can affect a creature's versatility and solace. Veterinary muscular experts use experiences from cranial life structures to analyze and deal with conditions like joint inflammation, cracks, and joint anomalies.

3. **Crossing point of Fields: Near Life systems and Morphometrics**

The crossing point of cranial examinations with fossil science and veterinary science is exemplified in the field of near life systems and morphometrics. Near life systems includes the deliberate examination of likenesses and contrasts in the designs of various species, giving a premise to grasping transformative connections. Morphometrics, then again, quantitatively dissects the size and state of organic designs, taking into consideration factual correlations.

Analysts in both fossil science and veterinary science use similar life systems to draw matches among species and deduce developmental connections. By applying morphometric procedures to cranial examinations, researchers can quantitatively evaluate varieties in cranial highlights inside and across species. This approach works with the recognizable proof of versatile patterns, transformative examples, and recognizes individual and species-level contrasts.

Chapter 8

Conservation Implications

Cranial investigations, enveloping the nitty gritty assessment of the skulls and related designs of different species, have sweeping ramifications for preservation endeavors. Past their importance in understanding physical variations and transformative cycles, cranial examinations contribute significant experiences that straightforwardly illuminate protection techniques. This far reaching investigation digs into the multilayered protection ramifications of cranial examinations, tending to how the information got from these investigations can be applied to safeguard biodiversity and keep up with environment wellbeing.

II. Cranial Transformations and Biological system Elements

1. **Specialty Specialization**

   Cranial transformations are complicatedly connected to the environmental specialties involved by various species. Understanding the subtleties of cranial designs gives environmentalists experiences into how species interface with their surroundings, including their jobs as hunters, herbivores, or omnivores. Moderates influence this information to recognize key species inside biological systems and configuration designated protection drives that focus on the safeguarding of these crucial entertainers.

2. **Trophic Communications**

The investigation of cranial life structures supports unraveling trophic cooperations inside environments. By looking at the skull morphology of hunters and prey, specialists can evaluate the coevolutionary elements that shape these connections. Protectionists use this data to address irregular characteristics in trophic fountains brought about by variables like natural surroundings misfortune or the presentation of obtrusive species. Reestablishing normal trophic associations is vital for keeping up with biological system steadiness.

III. Preservation of Undermined and Jeopardized Species

1. **Recognizing Species In danger**
   Cranial examinations assume a critical part in recognizing species that are especially defenseless against natural dangers. By examining the cranial attributes of different species, researchers can pinpoint those with particular transformations or restricted appropriations. This data is urgent for focusing on protection endeavors and apportioning assets to shield the most jeopardized species.
2. **Populace Wellbeing Evaluation**

The soundness of populaces can be surveyed through the assessment of cranial designs. Cranial anomalies, frequently demonstrative of natural stressors or hereditary issues, can be recognized through cautious investigation. Traditionalists utilize this data to screen the prosperity of populaces in the wild, empowering designated mediations when important. Such wellbeing appraisals add to the general administration of jeopardized species and help in forestalling populace declines.

IV. Protection Hereditary qualities and Cranial Attributes

1. **Hereditary Variety and Cranial Highlights**
   Cranial qualities are impacted by natural elements as well as by basic hereditary components. Protection hereditary qualities, combined with cranial investigations, permits scientists to investigate the hereditary variety inside populaces. Recognizing key qualities related with cranial transformations empowers a more profound comprehension of the innate premise of these characteristics. This information is fundamental for forming protection methodologies that focus on the conservation of hereditary variety.
2. **Inbreeding and Cranial Oddities**

In little and separated populaces, inbreeding can prompt the declaration of malicious attributes, including cranial abnormalities. Cranial examinations add to the ID of such peculiarities, filling in as signs of possible hereditary issues inside populaces. Progressives can utilize this data to execute hereditary administration procedures, like movements or hostage reproducing programs, to relieve the adverse consequences of inbreeding and improve the by and large hereditary strength of populaces.

V. Natural surroundings Preservation and Rebuilding

1. **Natural Reclamation**
   Cranial examinations give significant data about the environmental jobs of species inside their territories. This information is instrumental in planning and executing living space rebuilding drives. By understanding the particular cranial transformations that empower species to flourish in their common habitats, moderates can make reclamation designs that help the restoration of useful environments.

2. Scene Availability

Cranial examinations add to the ID of scene highlights critical for species development and relocation. Keeping up with scene availability is indispensable for the hereditary variety and long haul endurance of populaces.

Preservation drives informed by cranial examinations center around protecting and upgrading passages that work with the development of species, forestalling natural surroundings discontinuity and guaranteeing the practicality of interconnected environments.

VI. Environmental Change and Cranial Versatility

1. Versatile Reactions to Environmental Change

As environmental change modifies natural circumstances, species should adjust to new difficulties. Cranial examinations empower researchers to evaluate the flexibility of species by looking at authentic variations kept in skull morphology. Preservation methodologies can be created in view of a comprehension of how species have adapted to past natural changes, directing endeavors to help their flexibility notwithstanding contemporary environment challenges.

2. Prescient Displaying

Cranial information, when coordinated with environment demonstrating, works with prescient evaluations of how species could answer future environment situations. Preservationists utilize these prescient models to distinguish locales where species are probably going to confront expanded dangers or where new open doors for protection might emerge. This forward-looking methodology considers proactive protection arranging fully expecting environment actuated shifts in species disseminations.

VII. Public Mindfulness and Training

1. Imparting Preservation Messages

Cranial investigations offer enrapturing accounts of transformation and endurance that resound with the general population. Progressives influence these stories to convey the significance of biodiversity and the interconnectedness of environments. Drawing in tales about extraordinary cranial transformations, for example, those connected with taking care of procedures or correspondence, act as incredible assets for bringing issues to light about the benefit of safeguarding different species.

2. Instructive Projects

Integrating cranial examinations into instructive projects improves public comprehension of the complex connections between life systems, nature, and preservation. By encouraging an appreciation for the job of cranial transformations in molding species' communications with their surroundings, instructive drives add to a more educated and naturally cognizant society. This mindfulness is basic for accumulating public help for preservation endeavors.

VIII. Challenges and Moral Contemplations

1. **Moral Utilization of Cranial Information**

   While cranial examinations offer significant experiences, moral contemplations should direct their utilization. Preservationists should guarantee that examination rehearses are conscious of individual creatures and populaces. The dependable assortment and utilization of cranial information, especially with regards to studies including live creatures, expect adherence to moral principles to limit likely mischief and stress to the subjects.

2. **Coordinating Native Information**

Protection endeavors informed by cranial examinations ought to be comprehensive of native information frameworks. Native people group frequently have important bits of knowledge into the connections among species and their surroundings. Coordinating native points of view improves the viability of protection systems, cultivating cooperative methodologies that regard assorted approaches to understanding and associating with nature.

8.1 Discussing how understanding cranial anatomy aids in conservation efforts.

Preservation endeavors are complicatedly connected to how we might interpret the life systems and physiology of the species we try to safeguard. Among the bunch features of organic review, cranial life systems arises as a key part in protection science. This conversation dives into the manners by which grasping cranial life systems helps protection endeavors, investigating the important experiences it gives across different components of biodiversity safeguarding.

1. **Cranial Life structures as an Outline for Usefulness**
1. **Taking care of Procedures and Transformations**

   Cranial life structures fills in as an outline for the usefulness of a living being, particularly regarding taking care of methodologies. Various species show amazing variations in their skulls that are custom-made to their dietary inclinations. For example, the shape and construction of the skull can uncover whether a creature is herbivorous, predatory, or omnivorous. Understanding these transformations is fundamental for making preservation techniques that guarantee the accessibility of reasonable food sources inside safeguarded territories.

2. **Specialty Specialization**

Cranial variations frequently mirror the natural specialty an animal types possesses. By examining the cranial highlights of an animal types, moderates can acquire experiences into its job inside a biological system.

This information is pivotal for recognizing cornerstone species that assume lopsidedly enormous parts in keeping up with biodiversity and environment balance. Preservation endeavors can then be decisively coordinated towards saving environments that help these specific specialties.

II. Signs of Wellbeing and Populace Elements

1. Biomarkers of Ecological Pressure

The soundness of populaces is unpredictably attached to the state of their cranial designs. Cranial anomalies, going from dental issues to disfigurements, can act as biomarkers of ecological stressors. Moderates utilize these markers to survey the general prosperity of populaces and to recognize possible dangers, like contamination, natural surroundings debasement, or environmental change. Early identification of these stressors takes into account designated intercessions to alleviate their effects.

2. Observing Hereditary Variety

Cranial examinations add to observing hereditary variety inside populaces. Hereditary variety is reflected in cranial qualities, and concentrating on these characteristics supports recognizing levels of variety inside a populace. This data is significant for preservationists as it guides choices connected with rearing projects, movements, and territory the executives. Keeping up with hereditary variety is fundamental for the drawn out strength of populaces despite changing natural circumstances.

III. Preservation Hereditary qualities and Cranial Attributes

1. Hereditary Premise of Cranial Elements

Cranial qualities are not exclusively formed by natural elements; they likewise have a hereditary premise. Understanding the hereditary underpinnings of cranial highlights is urgent for preservation hereditary qualities. Scientists can distinguish explicit qualities related with transformations basic for an animal categories' endurance. This hereditary data improves our capacity to foster designated preservation methodologies that mean to safeguard the outward morphology as well as the fundamental hereditary variety fundamental for variation.

2. Distinguishing Inbreeding and Hereditary Oddities

Inbreeding inside little populaces can prompt the statement of malicious attributes, including cranial peculiarities. Cranial examinations give a method for distinguishing such oddities, filling in as early advance notice indications of likely hereditary issues inside populaces. Traditionalists can then execute techniques to address inbreeding, for example, presenting hereditary variety through movements or oversaw rearing projects, guaranteeing the drawn out reasonability of populaces.

IV. Surveying Biological system Wellbeing and Usefulness

1. **Trophic Collaborations and Food Networks**

   Cranial investigations add to how we might interpret trophic connections inside environments. By analyzing the cranial morphology of hunters and prey, researchers can unwind the mind boggling connections that shape food networks. Protection endeavors can focus on the safeguarding of these trophic communications, guaranteeing that the departure of a solitary animal categories doesn't set off flowing impacts that upset the equilibrium of whole environments.

2. **Territory Reclamation and Useful Jobs**

The experiences acquired from cranial examinations help in planning compelling territory reclamation drives. Understanding the utilitarian jobs of species inside their environments permits moderates to focus on the renewed introduction of key species that add to biological system wellbeing. By zeroing in on the reclamation of useful variety, protection endeavors become more nuanced and lined up with the regular cycles that support environments.

V. Environmental Change Variation Systems

1. **Authentic Transformations as Indicators**

   Cranial investigations offer a window into the verifiable transformations of species to changing ecological circumstances. By dissecting cranial highlights, researchers can recognize how species have answered past environment variances. This verifiable viewpoint turns into a significant instrument for foreseeing how species could adjust to future environmental change. Preservation techniques can then integrate proactive measures in view of a comprehension of an animal varieties' versatile potential.

2. **Preservation Making arrangements for Environment Actuated Movements**

As environmental change adjusts territories, species circulations are supposed to move. Cranial examinations help in anticipating these movements and arranging preservation endeavors likewise. Recognizing districts where species are probably going to confront expanded dangers or on the other hand, regions where new living spaces might become reasonable, takes into consideration expectant preservation arranging. This forward-looking methodology is fundamental for alleviating the effects of environmental change on biodiversity.

VI. Public Mindfulness and Schooling

1. **Displaying Biodiversity's Wonders**
   Cranial investigations offer charming accounts of variation and endurance that can be incredible assets for public commitment. By exhibiting the wonders of biodiversity through cranial transformations, preservationists can ingrain a feeling of marvel and appreciation for the complex snare of life. Public mindfulness crusades that influence cranial investigations add to building a voting demographic that qualities and effectively upholds preservation drives.
2. **Instructive Projects and Resident Science**

Coordinating cranial investigations into instructive projects upgrades public comprehension of the interconnectedness between life systems, environment, and preservation. Resident science drives that include people in general in gathering cranial information, like following natural life populaces or observing cranial peculiarities, give a scaffold between logical exploration and local area commitment. Schooling turns into an impetus for grassroots protection endeavors.

VII. Challenges and Moral Contemplations

1. **Adjusting Exploration Needs and Moral Practices**
   While cranial examinations give significant experiences, it is basic to offset research needs with moral practices. Traditionalists should guarantee that examination strategies are harmless and focus on the government assistance of individual creatures. Moral contemplations reach out to the treatment of examples, the utilization of innovation, and the scattering of discoveries to guarantee that the advantages of cranial investigations are accomplished without compromising the prosperity of the concentrated on species.
2. **Social Awareness and Native Information**

Cranial examinations ought to be led with social responsiveness, particularly in areas where native networks hold profound associations with the concentrated on species. Incorporating native information frameworks into cranial investigations upgrades the adequacy of protection endeavors. Joint effort with native networks guarantees that protection methodologies regard customary environmental information and encourage a comprehensive way to deal with biodiversity safeguarding.

VIII. Future Bearings and Innovative Advances

1. **Mechanical Developments in Imaging**
   Headways in imaging advances, for example, higher-goal sweeps and continuous imaging modalities, keep on refining our capacity to concentrate on cranial life systems. These developments guarantee considerably more noteworthy lucidity in unwinding the complexities of cranial designs.
   Harmless methods like compact CT scanners and high level microscopy open

new roads for field research, empowering moderates to assemble information with insignificant interruption to untamed life.

2. **Coordinating Multi-disciplinary Methodologies**

The eventual fate of cranial examinations in preservation lies in coordinating multi-disciplinary methodologies. Coordinated effort between geneticists, scientists, anthropologists, and preservation researcher cultivates an all encompassing comprehension of cranial transformations and their suggestions for protection. This interdisciplinary cooperative energy takes into consideration a more exhaustive and nuanced way to deal with tending to the perplexing difficulties looked by biodiversity.

8.2 The role of genetic diversity in maintaining healthy cranial features.

The complex woven artwork of life appears in the surprising variety of cranial elements among various species. At the core of this variety lies the hereditary code, coordinating the turn of events and support of cranial designs. The job of hereditary variety in supporting sound cranial highlights is a diverse and crucial part of transformative science and protection science. This conversation investigates the interaction between hereditary variety and cranial wellbeing, revealing insight into its suggestions for species endurance and biological system flexibility.

1. **The Hereditary Outline of Cranial Highlights**

1. **Formative Starting points**

   The outline for cranial elements is engraved in the hereditary material of every species. During undeveloped turn of events, qualities organize the arrangement of cranial designs, deciding the size, shape, and usefulness of the skull. Varieties in these qualities add to the variety saw across species, reflecting variations to various conditions, natural specialties, and transformative tensions.

2. **Legacy and Variety**

Hereditary variety, the consequence of varieties in the DNA succession among people inside a populace, assumes a critical part in forming cranial elements. Legacy designs oversee the transmission of hereditary data starting with one age then onto the next. Changeability in qualities presents variety in cranial characteristics, adding to the versatility of species to their particular living spaces and ways of life.

II. Keeping up with Versatile Attributes

1. **Transformative Elements**

   Hereditary variety is the fuel of transformative cycles, driving the rise of versatile qualities that present benefits in unambiguous conditions. Cranial highlights frequently advance because of biological tensions, for example, changes in food sources, contest for assets, or changes in environment. Hereditary variety guarantees that populaces harbor a range of characteristics, working with variation to dynamic ecological circumstances and keeping up with the wellness of an animal categories.

2. **Preservation of Versatile Potential**

Safeguarding hereditary variety is vital for saving the versatile possible encoded in cranial highlights. Populaces with higher hereditary variety have a more extensive scope of characteristics, improving their ability to answer ecological difficulties. Protection endeavors that focus on keeping up with hereditary variety assist with defending the versatile munititions stockpile inside populaces, guaranteeing they can endure changing circumstances and developing dangers.

III. Hereditary Variety and Cranial Wellbeing

1. **Decreasing the Gamble of Injurious Qualities**

   Hereditary variety fills in as a characteristic cushion against the outflow of harmful qualities. In little, detached populaces with restricted hereditary variety, the gamble of acquired messes and cranial irregularities increments. A different genetic supply diminishes the probability of latent hereditary problems becoming manifest, adding to generally speaking cranial wellbeing inside populaces.

2. **Staying away from Inbreeding Misery**

Inbreeding, the mating of firmly related people, can prompt inbreeding melancholy — a decrease in wellness because of the statement of unsafe latent alleles. Keeping up with hereditary variety limits the event of inbreeding melancholy, forestalling the appearance of cranial anomalies and saving the general soundness of populaces.

IV. Populace Level Effects

1. **Infection Opposition**

   Hereditary variety is a vital consider infection opposition inside populaces. A different genetic supply gives the natural substance to the improvement of insusceptible reactions that can battle a scope of microorganisms. Cranial wellbeing is firmly connected to the general strength of people, and hereditary variety adds to the flexibility of populaces against illnesses that can influence cranial designs, like those affecting dental wellbeing or causing bone deformations.

2. **Natural Flexibility**

Hereditary variety improves a populace's capacity to adjust to changing natural circumstances. This versatility is essential for keeping up with cranial wellbeing, particularly notwithstanding difficulties, for example, natural surroundings corruption, environmental change, or changes in asset accessibility. Populaces with high hereditary variety are better prepared to change their cranial elements to line up with developing biological elements.

V. Preservation Methodologies for Hereditary Variety and Cranial Wellbeing

1. **Living space Availability**
   Safeguarding hereditary variety requires keeping up with availability between populaces. Living space fracture disturbs the normal development of people, prompting separated populaces with decreased hereditary trade. Laying out and keeping up with halls that work with the development of people between living spaces advances quality stream, supporting hereditary variety and, thus, cranial wellbeing.

2. **Movements and Hereditary Administration**

Protectionists utilize movement techniques to acquaint hereditary variety with little or segregated populaces. By bringing people from hereditarily particular populaces, movements infuse new hereditary material, decreasing the gamble of inbreeding and advancing cranial wellbeing. Hereditary administration plans, informed by cranial examinations, guide these endeavors to guarantee the safeguarding of versatile characteristics.

VI. Cranial Elements as Marks of Hereditary Wellbeing

1. **Cranial Abnormalities as Advance notice Signs**
   Cranial elements can act as apparent signs of hereditary wellbeing inside populaces. Peculiarities or disfigurements in skulls might flag basic hereditary issues, including inbreeding or the declaration of malicious alleles. Moderates utilize cranial investigations to screen and evaluate the commonness of abnormalities, giving experiences into the hereditary strength of populaces.

2. **Observing Hereditary Changes After some time**

Long haul cranial investigations empower analysts to screen hereditary changes inside populaces after some time. Following varieties in cranial highlights can uncover shifts in hereditary variety, variation to new ecological circumstances, or the effects of human-prompted changes. This continuous observing guides in changing preservation techniques to address arising hereditary difficulties and guarantee the supported soundness of cranial elements.

VII. Challenges and Moral Contemplations

1. **Adjusting Hereditary Mediation and Regular Cycles**
   While hereditary administration procedures can be compelling, they should be offset with a comprehension of normal transformative cycles. Traditionalists face the test of deciding when and how to mediate to keep up with hereditary variety

without disturbing the inborn elements of populaces. Moral contemplations guide choices to guarantee mediations line up with the drawn out wellbeing and suitability of species.

2. **Social Awareness**

Hereditary variety preservation endeavors ought to be drawn nearer with social awareness, particularly while working with native networks. Incorporating conventional biological information into hereditary administration plans recognizes the comprehensive points of view of native societies and cultivates cooperative methodologies that regard both hereditary variety and social variety.

VIII. Future Headings: Incorporating Hereditary qualities and Cranial Examinations

1. **Propels in Hereditary Advances**
   Proceeded with headways in hereditary advancements hold guarantee for refining how we might interpret the transaction between hereditary variety and cranial highlights. High-throughput sequencing, extensive affiliation studies, and high level hereditary planning strategies offer uncommon bits of knowledge into the hereditary premise of cranial variations. Coordinating these advancements with cranial investigations will extend our appreciation of the nuanced connections among qualities and cranial wellbeing.

2. **Multi-disciplinary Methodologies**

The eventual fate of understanding hereditary variety and cranial wellbeing lies in multi-disciplinary methodologies. Coordinated effort between geneticists, cranial anatomists, protection scientists, and environmentalists cultivates an all encompassing viewpoint. This mix of skill empowers an extensive comprehension of what hereditary variety means for cranial highlights and, thusly, how cranial wellbeing adds to the general wellness and versatility of populaces.

8.3 Challenges and opportunities in preserving lion populations.

Lions, the notable dominant hunters of the African savannas, face a horde of difficulties compromising their endurance. At the same time, a scope of chances exists to relieve these dangers and cultivate the preservation of lion populaces. This conversation investigates the complicated scene of difficulties and open doors in saving these superb huge felines.

1. **Challenges Confronting Lion Populaces**
1. **Natural surroundings Misfortune and Discontinuity**
   One of the premier difficulties for lions is the misfortune and discontinuity of their regular natural surroundings. Human infringement, driven by farming, framework improvement, and urbanization, has essentially diminished the

immense regions lions expect to flourish. Divided environments present snags to quality stream between populaces, prompting hereditary confinement and expanding the weakness of nearby gatherings.

2. **Human-Natural life Struggle**

As human populaces venture into lion regions, clashes emerge. Lions might go after animals, prompting counter from neighborhood networks. The resultant human-untamed life struggle imperils lions as well as fills negative insights, putting forth preservation attempts seriously testing. Tending to these struggles requires a sensitive harmony between safeguarding nearby livelihoods and preserving lion populaces.

3. **Poaching and Unlawful Untamed life Exchange**

Poaching stays a steady danger to lion populaces. While lions are not focused on for their body parts as every now and again as a few different animal types, they frequently succumb to catches planned for different creatures. Moreover, the unlawful natural life exchange, driven by interest for lion bones and other body parts in customary medication, represents a danger to their endurance.

4. **Environmental Change**

Environmental change presents new difficulties for lions. Modified precipitation examples and temperature limits can affect prey accessibility and upset biological systems. Lions, adjusted to explicit climatic circumstances, may confront provokes in acclimating to these quick ecological changes, influencing their circulation and overflow.

5. **Infection Episodes**

Infection episodes, like canine sickness and cow-like tuberculosis, can annihilate lion populaces. These illnesses frequently spill over from homegrown creatures, underlining the interconnectedness among natural life and homegrown animals. Alleviating infection dangers requires comprehensive methodologies that address both natural life and homegrown creature wellbeing.

II. Open doors for Preservation

1. **Safeguarded Regions and Passage Creation**

Laying out and keeping up with safeguarded regions act as crucial apparatuses for lion preservation. These regions give asylums where lions can wander, chase, and breed without direct dangers from human exercises.

Making untamed life halls between these safeguarded regions works with quality stream, diminishing the dangers related with hereditary detachment.

2. **Local area Based Protection**

Drawing in neighborhood networks in lion preservation is a strong open door. Local area based preservation drives enable nearby inhabitants to become stewards of their normal legacy. By giving impetuses to conjunction, for example, remuneration for animals misfortunes and ecotourism benefits, networks become accomplices in lion protection as opposed to foes.

3. **Against Poaching Measures**

Strong enemy of poaching endeavors are critical for defending lion populaces. This incorporates expanded watching, sending of innovation, for example, robots and camera traps, and joint effort with policing. Focusing on the unlawful untamed life exchange through tough authorization measures can control the interest for lion items.

4. **Environment Flexibility Systems**

Preservation systems need to coordinate environment flexibility measures. This includes understanding what environmental change means for lion territories and prey accessibility. Executing versatile administration rehearses, like natural surroundings rebuilding and water asset the executives, can upgrade the flexibility of lion populaces notwithstanding environment related difficulties.

5. **Infection Checking and The executives**

Consistent checking and the executives of sicknesses influencing lion populaces are fundamental. Cooperative endeavors between natural life veterinarians, scientists, and neighborhood networks can assist with executing immunization programs for homegrown creatures and moderate sickness overflow. This coordinated methodology advances the soundness of both natural life and domesticated animals.

III. All encompassing Protection Methodologies

1. **Environment Based Protection**

Embracing an environment based protection approach perceives that lions are important for complex biological systems. Safeguarding lions alone is inadequate; shielding their prey species, keeping up with biodiversity, and protecting generally speaking biological system wellbeing add to the drawn out endurance of lion populaces.

2. **Exploration and Innovation**

Putting resources into exploration and innovation is critical for informed protection independent direction. Headways in following advances, hereditary qualities, and environmental demonstrating give significant experiences into lion conduct, populace elements, and natural surroundings necessities. This information guides protection procedures and upgrades how we might interpret the multifaceted variables affecting lion populaces.

3. **Training and Mindfulness**

Training and mindfulness drives assume an essential part in building public help for lion protection. Drawing in nearby networks, policymakers, and the worldwide public cultivates a feeling of obligation and supports reasonable practices. Moreover, encouraging a more profound comprehension of lions' environmental jobs and social importance dissipates misinterpretations and supports conjunction endeavors.

IV. Worldwide Coordinated effort

1. **Transboundary Preservation Endeavors**
   Lion populaces frequently stretch out past public boundaries, accentuating the requirement for transboundary preservation drives. Cooperative endeavors between adjoining nations guarantee an organized way to deal with lion preservation. Shared research, data trade, and joint protection techniques add to the safeguarding of bigger, hereditarily different populaces.

2. **Worldwide Associations**

Worldwide associations and backing are instrumental in tending to the complex difficulties confronting lion populaces. Worldwide associations, NGOs, and administrative offices can give financing, aptitude, and backing to reinforce neighborhood preservation drives. A brought together worldwide exertion is fundamental for handling issues, for example, the unlawful untamed life exchange and environmental change, which rise above public limits.

V. Moral Contemplations in Protection

1. **Regard for Native Information**
   Regarding and coordinating native information into preservation methodologies is crucial. Native people group frequently have priceless bits of knowledge into neighborhood environments and natural life conduct. Cooperative methodologies that recognize and consolidate conventional insight upgrade the adequacy and social awareness of protection endeavors.

2. **Moral The travel industry Practices**

The travel industry can be a blade that cuts both ways for lion preservation. On one hand, all around oversaw ecotourism can give monetary advantages and encourage appreciation for natural life. Then again, flighty the travel industry practices can upset lion conduct and territories. Taking on moral the travel industry rules guarantees that preservation endeavors line up with standards of insignificant effect and maintainability.

Chapter 9

Future Directions In Cranial Anatomy Research

Cranial life systems research remains at the front of figuring out the perplexing designs that shape the heads of assorted organic entities. As innovation develops and interdisciplinary joint efforts expand, the eventual fate of cranial life structures research guarantees momentous headways. This far reaching investigation dives into the expected directions and arising topics that could shape the following period of cranial life systems research.

1. **Mechanical Advances and Imaging Developments**
1. **High-Goal Imaging Procedures**

   Future examination in cranial life systems is probably going to observe a flood in high-goal imaging strategies. Advances like miniature figured tomography (miniature CT) and attractive reverberation imaging (X-ray) keep on propelling, offering phenomenal lucidity in envisioning inner cranial designs. The capacity to painlessly inspect mind boggling subtleties at the miniature level opens new roads for concentrating on physical variations with unrivaled accuracy.

2. **Three-Layered Displaying and Virtual Analyzations**

   The joining of three-layered (3D) displaying and virtual analyzations is ready to alter the manner in which specialists investigate cranial life systems. Virtual recreations, made from imaging information, empower researchers to take apart and control cranial designs carefully. This approach improves instructive assets as well as works with inside and out examinations of utilitarian morphology and biomechanics without the requirement for actual examples.

3. **Progresses in Utilitarian Imaging**

Practical imaging strategies, like useful X-ray (fMRI) and positron discharge tomography (PET), hold guarantee for unwinding the powerful parts of cranial life systems. These advancements can catch continuous changes in blood stream, brain movement, and metabolic cycles, offering bits of knowledge into how cranial designs answer during different capabilities like taking care of, correspondence, and tangible discernment.

II. Incorporating Atomic and Hereditary Methodologies

1. **Genomic Experiences into Cranial Advancement**
   The marriage of cranial life systems research with genomics opens new outskirts in grasping the hereditary premise of cranial advancement. Near genomics can explain the qualities liable for cranial variations, offering a sub-atomic viewpoint on the hidden hereditary systems molding different cranial structures. This integrative methodology upgrades our understanding of how hereditary varieties add to morphological variety.

2. **Epigenetics and Cranial Turn of events**
   Investigating the job of epigenetics in cranial improvement is a prospering area of examination. Epigenetic changes, which impact quality articulation without modifying the basic DNA grouping, assume a significant part in molding cranial designs. Exploring epigenetic guideline during undeveloped turn of events and all through a creature's life can give bits of knowledge into the natural elements affecting cranial aggregates.

3. **Transformative Formative Science (Evo-Devotional) of the Skull**

The field of transformative formative science, or Evo-Devotional, is ready to offer significant bits of knowledge into the advancement of cranial designs. Concentrating on the formative cycles that lead to the development of the skull across various species gives an all encompassing comprehension of the hereditary and sub-atomic underpinnings of cranial variety. Near Evo-Devotional investigations can unwind rationed and dissimilar formative pathways.

III. Practical Morphology and Biomechanics

1. **Computational Demonstrating for Useful Investigations**
   Progressions in computational displaying and reenactment procedures will assume a crucial part in unwinding the utilitarian parts of cranial life systems. Limited component investigation (FEA) and biomechanical demonstrating permit specialists to mimic the mechanical ways of behaving of cranial designs under different circumstances. This approach supports understanding how structure connects with capability, giving experiences into the versatile meaning of cranial elements.

2. **Biomechanics of Taking care of and Prey Catch**
   Future examination in cranial life structures is probably going to dig further into the biomechanics of taking care of, especially in meat eating species like lions. Concentrating on the practical parts of the jaw, teeth, and cranial muscle structure during prey catch gives fundamental data on how cranial

transformations work with productive hunting and taking care of techniques. This information has suggestions for understanding hunter prey elements and environmental jobs.

3. Sensorimotor Mix and Neurobiology

Investigating sensorimotor mix and the neurobiology of cranial designs is a blossoming road. Examining how tactile data is handled and coordinated inside the skull, particularly in species with specific variations, offers bits of knowledge into the advancement of tangible organs. This interdisciplinary methodology spans neuroscience and cranial life systems, revealing the brain premise of cranial capabilities.

IV. Developmental Importance and Variations

1. Paleontological Bits of knowledge into Cranial Advancement

The incorporation of paleontological strategies with current methods holds enormous potential for recreating the developmental history of cranial designs. Fossilized skulls give previews of past morphologies, and advances in imaging and logical devices empower analysts to extricate definite data from old examples. This interdisciplinary methodology offers a worldly aspect to how we might interpret cranial development.

2. Transformative Morphometrics and Shape Examination

The fate of cranial life structures research includes refining morphometric and shape investigation strategies. Mathematical morphometrics, a technique that evaluates shape varieties, can be applied across different taxa to investigate developmental examples. Incorporating developmental morphometrics with atomic information takes into account more vigorous recreations of phylogenetic connections and versatile radiations.

3. Natural Transformations and Biological Specialty

Understanding how cranial transformations connect with natural changes and biological specialties is a urgent road for future exploration. Examining how cranial designs advance because of movements in environment, territory, and accessible assets gives bits of knowledge into the versatile methodologies of species. This information is especially important for anticipating how species might answer continuous ecological changes.

V. Applied Exploration in Preservation and Medication

1. Cranial Pathologies and Preservation Wellbeing

Applied research in cranial life structures reaches out to concentrating on pathologies and abnormalities, especially with regards to preservation wellbeing. Distinguishing normal cranial pathologies in both hostage and wild populaces illuminates veterinary practices and adds to the general prosperity of species under protection the executives. This information helps with alleviating well-being challenges and advancing populace strength.

2. **Protection Hereditary qualities and Cranial Attributes**

   Coordinating protection hereditary qualities with cranial examinations offers practical applications for species preservation. Recognizing key cranial characteristics related with hereditary variety illuminates hereditary administration systems. Progressives can utilize cranial information to direct movements, hostage rearing projects, and environment rebuilding drives that intend to safeguard both morphological and hereditary variety inside populaces.

3. **Clinical Applications and Biomimicry**

The investigation of cranial life systems is progressively impacting clinical applications and biomimicry. Experiences into cranial designs, like the complexities of the human skull, motivate developments in clinical imaging, careful methods, and prosthetics. Biomimicry, drawing motivation from nature's plans, can prompt the advancement of bio-propelled materials and designs with applications in different fields.

VI. Moral Contemplations and Social Responsiveness

1. **Moral Utilization of Examples and Information**

   As cranial life systems research progresses, moral contemplations should direct the assortment and utilization of examples and information. Scientists should focus on the moral treatment of examples, guaranteeing mindful assortment rehearses and deferential taking care of. Straightforward correspondence with people in general about the moral ramifications of cranial examination encourages trust and understanding.

2. **Social Awareness in Cranial Examinations**

Cranial investigations ought to be led with social awareness, particularly while working with native networks. Recognizing and regarding social points of view on the utilization of examples and the investigation of cranial life structures is fundamental. Cooperative endeavors that include native information holders add to more all encompassing and socially comprehensive exploration rehearses.

VII. Interdisciplinary Coordinated efforts and Information Reconciliation

1. **Interdisciplinary Exploration Groups**

   The eventual fate of cranial life systems research lies in cultivating interdisciplinary joint efforts. Uniting specialists from fields like hereditary qualities, environment, human sciences, fossil science, and medication upgrades the profundity and expansiveness of cranial investigations. Cooperative exploration groups can handle complex inquiries that range various disciplines, giving extensive bits of knowledge into the complexities of cranial life structures.

2. Information Coordination Stages

Propels in information combination stages will work with the union of information from assorted sources. Stages that permit specialists to flawlessly coordinate physical, hereditary, biological, and biomechanical information offer a comprehensive comprehension of cranial designs. Such combination is vital for unwinding the intricate connections between structure, capability, and transformative history.

VIII. Public Commitment and Science Correspondence

1. Public Mindfulness Missions

As cranial life structures research advances, public commitment becomes vital. Imparting the meaning of cranial examinations to the more extensive public improves mindfulness and appreciation for biodiversity. Public mindfulness missions can grandstand the wonders of cranial variations, encouraging an association between logical revelations and public interest in the normal world.

2. Instructive Effort Projects

Instructive effort programs assume a critical part in molding the up and coming age of cranial anatomists and moderates. Coordinating cranial life structures into school educational plans, gallery displays, and intuitive projects sparkles interest and interest in the natural sciences. Instructive drives likewise add to developing an experimentally educated society that qualities and supports progressing research endeavors.

IX. Subsidizing and Backing for Cranial Life structures Exploration

1. Research Awards and Financing Drives

Supporting the force in cranial life structures research needs vigorous monetary help. Research awards and subsidizing drives, both from legislative and non-administrative sources, assume a basic part in progressing logical examinations. Financing potential open doors ought to focus on projects that line up with preservation objectives, clinical applications, and interdisciplinary coordinated efforts.

2. Humanitarian Help and Corporate Associations

Humanitarian help and corporate associations present extra roads for reinforcing cranial life systems research. Humanitarian associations with a guarantee to biodiversity preservation, medical services, and logical investigation can contribute essentially to progressing cranial examinations. Corporate associations can offer assets, innovation, and mastery to drive advancement in cranial life systems research.

9.1 Emerging areas of study and research opportunities.

The field of natural sciences is dynamic and consistently advancing, with scientists continually pushing the limits of information. As innovation progresses and interdisciplinary joint efforts prosper, intriguing areas of study arise, offering an abundance of examination open doors. This investigation digs into probably the most encouraging and inventive spaces inside natural sciences, giving a brief look into the eventual fate of examination.

1. **Genomic Medication and Accuracy Wellbeing**
1. **Genomic The study of disease transmission**
   The mix of genomics into epidemiological examinations is changing comprehension we might interpret sickness elements. Genomic the study of disease transmission joins conventional epidemiological techniques with cutting edge genomic sequencing to follow the spread of irresistible sicknesses, disentangle their hereditary underpinnings, and illuminate designated general wellbeing intercessions. Research in this space holds monstrous potential for controlling episodes, anticipating sickness patterns, and creating customized therapy techniques.
2. **Accuracy Oncology**

Accuracy oncology is reforming malignant growth treatment by fitting treatments to the novel hereditary cosmetics of individual patients' cancers. Propels in genomic sequencing advancements permit analysts to distinguish explicit hereditary changes driving disease movement. Examining the sub-atomic and hereditary premise of malignant growth empowers the improvement of designated treatments, further developing treatment results and limiting incidental effects. The advancing scene of accuracy oncology offers various examination roads, from understanding opposition systems to investigating novel restorative targets.

II. Neuroscience and Mind Exploration

1. **Brain adaptability and Mental Upgrade**
   The investigation of brain adaptability — the cerebrum's capacity to rearrange itself — opens new outskirts in figuring out mental upgrade. Specialists investigate intercessions, like mental preparation, neurostimulation, and pharmacological methodologies, to bridle the mind's versatility for upgrading learning, memory, and mental capability. Unwinding the instruments of brain adaptability gives bits of knowledge into neurological problems and offers open doors for creating intercessions to improve mental capacities across various populaces.
2. **Connectomics and Mind Planning**
3. Progressions in connectomics, the thorough planning of brain associations in the mind, empower specialists to make nitty gritty cerebrum map books. High-goal imaging strategies, joined with computational examinations, take

into account the perception of unpredictable brain circuits. Exploring the underlying and useful network of the cerebrum gives a more profound comprehension of neurodevelopmental messes, neurodegenerative infections, and the brain premise of conduct. The investigation of cerebrum connectomics is a quickly developing field with tremendous examination potential.

III. Microbiome and Microbial Environment

1. **Have Microbiome Cooperations**

   The human microbiome, containing trillions of microorganisms possessing the body, assumes a vital part in wellbeing and sickness. Research open doors have large amounts of understanding the perplexing collaborations between the host and its microbiota. Examinations concerning how the microbiome impacts digestion, safe capability, and neurological cycles offer roads for creating designated intercessions to tweak microbial networks for restorative purposes.

2. **Ecological Microbial Nature**

   Growing past the human microbiome, research in natural microbial biology investigates the variety and elements of microorganisms in different environments. From soil microbiomes to sea-going conditions, figuring out microbial networks' jobs in supplement cycling, bioremediation, and environment strength is a thriving region. Arising advancements, including metagenomics and single-cell sequencing, give phenomenal bits of knowledge into the tremendous microbial variety forming our planet.

IV. Manufactured Science and Bioengineering

1. **Genome Altering and CRISPR Advancements**

   The progressive CRISPR-Cas9 genome altering innovation keeps on catalyzing forward leaps in organic exploration. Research potential open doors in this field incorporate refining genome-altering methods, investigating novel CRISPR frameworks, and tending to moral contemplations. Applications range from creating quality treatments for hereditary problems to designing yields with improved flexibility and efficiency.

2. **Engineered Creatures and Xenobiology**

   The making of manufactured organic entities with designed hereditary codes extends the potential outcomes of life sciences. Xenobiology investigates the development of living beings with manufactured DNA, possibly opening new functionalities and applications.

   This interdisciplinary field meets with bioengineering, sub-atomic science, and manufactured science, offering novel examination roads in making counterfeit life structures for explicit purposes, for example, biofuel creation or ecological remediation.

V. Natural Preservation and Reclamation Biology

1. **Metropolitan Nature and Biodiversity in Urban areas**

   As urbanization speeds up all around the world, concentrating on biodiversity in metropolitan environments turns out to be progressively significant. Metropolitan biology researches how natural life adjusts to metropolitan conditions, the effect of urbanization on biodiversity, and procedures for advancing concurrence among people and natural life in urban areas. Research in this space adds to manageable metropolitan preparation, protection techniques, and the improvement of metropolitan biodiversity.

2. **Rebuilding Genomics**

   Rebuilding genomics consolidates genomics with biological reclamation practices to revive debased environments. Understanding the hereditary variety of plant and creature populaces in reclamation regions illuminates powerful protection methodologies. Specialists investigate how genomics can direct the determination of plant and creature species for reclamation projects, upgrade flexibility to ecological stressors, and advance the drawn out reasonability of reestablished biological systems.

VI. Arising Irresistible Illnesses and One Wellbeing

1. **Viral Development and Zoonotic Transmission**

   The continuous danger of arising irresistible illnesses, particularly those with zoonotic starting points, requires ceaseless examination endeavors. Exploring viral development, overflow occasions, and factors affecting zoonotic transmission upgrades our capacity to foresee and alleviate future pandemics. One Wellbeing draws near, coordinating human, creature, and natural wellbeing, give an all encompassing structure to understanding and tending to arising irresistible illnesses.

2. **Antimicrobial Obstruction and Medication Disclosure**

   Antimicrobial obstruction represents a worldwide wellbeing emergency, and research open doors have large amounts of figuring out the components of opposition and creating novel antimicrobial specialists. Research in drug revelation investigates creative methodologies, including the recognizable proof of new anti-microbial mixtures, reusing existing medications, and saddling the capability of phage treatment and immunotherapeutics to battle drug-safe microorganisms.

VII. Environmental Change Science and Transformation Systems

1. **Transformative Reactions to Environmental Change**
   Environmental change science explores how species adjust to quickly changing ecological circumstances. Research in this space investigates transformative reactions, phenotypic versatility, and hereditary variation in different creatures. Understanding how species adapt to environmental change illuminates protection techniques, predicts populace elements, and guides the advancement of versatile administration rehearses.
2. **Environment Versatile Horticulture and Yield Improvement**

   Environment strong farming is a squeezing research boondocks even with environmental change influences on food security. Creating crops with upgraded versatility to outrageous climate occasions, vermin, and it is foremost to change climatic circumstances. Research amazing open doors incorporate utilizing progressed rearing methods, utilizing genomics for crop improvement, and investigating manageable farming practices to guarantee worldwide food creation despite environment challenges.

VIII. Human Transformative Science and Human studies

1. **Paleogenomics and Old DNA Investigation**
   Headways in paleogenomics and old DNA examination have changed how we might interpret human advancement. Research open doors in this field incorporate remaking old human genomes, investigating populace elements, and exploring communications between hominin species. Experiences from paleogenomics add to unwinding the intricacies of human transformative history, relocation examples, and variation to assorted conditions.
2. **Social Development and Conduct Nature**

   Human transformative science stretches out past hereditary qualities to envelop social advancement and conduct nature. Research in this interdisciplinary field investigates how social practices, social designs, and natural elements have formed human social orders over the entire course of time. Examining the interchange among hereditary and social development gives an exhaustive comprehension of the versatile methodologies that have characterized the human species.

IX. Organic Information Science and Computational Science

1. **AI in Organic Information Examination**
   The reconciliation of AI strategies in organic information examination

is a prospering region. Specialists influence AI calculations to remove designs, anticipate natural results, and break down huge scope genomic datasets. Applications range from distinguishing sickness biomarkers to anticipating protein structures, offering groundbreaking open doors for information driven disclosures in the natural sciences.

2. **Network Science and Frameworks Science**

Network science and frameworks science approaches look at natural frameworks as interconnected organizations of particles and connections. Research open doors lie in demonstrating complex natural organizations, unraveling flagging pathways, and figuring out the emanant properties of organic frameworks. Coordinating information from genomics, proteomics, and metabolomics improves our appreciation of cell processes and their dysregulation in illnesses.

X. Bioethics and Cultural Ramifications of Natural Advances

1. **Moral Contemplations in Biomedical Exploration**
   As natural examination progresses, moral contemplations become fundamental. Bioethics investigates the moral ramifications of arising innovations, hereditary intercessions, and biomedical examination rehearses. Research open doors lie in creating moral structures, resolving issues of assent and security, and participating in broad daylight talk to guarantee dependable and evenhanded progressions in the existence sciences.

2. **Cultural Effects of Biotechnological Advancements**

Researching the cultural effects of biotechnological developments includes understanding how innovative progressions influence social orders. Research in this space investigates public discernments, social perspectives, and strategy ramifications of biotechnological leap forwards. Social researchers team up with scientists to guarantee that mechanical advancements line up with cultural qualities, moderate expected hurts, and contribute decidedly to worldwide prosperity.

XI. Interdisciplinary Coordinated efforts and Cross-Cutting Subjects

1. **Organic Sciences and Man-made consciousness Mix**
   The assembly of organic sciences with man-made brainpower (artificial intelligence) presents invigorating conceivable outcomes. Specialists investigate artificial intelligence applications in genomics, drug disclosure, biological demonstrating, and diagnostics. The collaboration between organic information and simulated intelligence calculations improves the speed and precision of examinations, opening up original exploration roads at the crossing point of science and computational sciences.

2. Translational Exploration and Seat to-Bedside Developments

Translational exploration overcomes any barrier between fundamental logical revelations and useful applications in medical services. Open doors have large amounts of making an interpretation of organic experiences into inventive treatments, diagnostics, and clinical mediations.

Specialists take part in seat to-bedside joint efforts to guarantee that logical disclosures have unmistakable advantages for patient consideration and general wellbeing.

9.2 Integrating technology and traditional methods for comprehensive insights.

In the steadily developing scene of examination and investigation, the reconciliation of innovation with customary techniques has turned into a groundbreaking worldview. This cooperative energy offers scientists a strong tool compartment, joining the qualities of laid out rehearses with the capacities of state of the art innovations. In this talk, we dive into the horde manners by which the coordination of innovation and customary techniques upgrades our grasping across different fields, from logical exploration to social conservation and then some.

1. Improving Logical Request

1. Information Obtaining and Accuracy in Estimation

In logical examination, the marriage of innovation and conventional strategies essentially hoists the accuracy and effectiveness of information obtaining. Advancements like sensors, robots, and satellite imaging supplement conventional hands on work, empowering analysts to accumulate broad information over huge regions and testing landscapes. This reconciliation facilitates the exploration cycle as well as upgrades the precision of estimations, giving a more far reaching comprehension of normal peculiarities.

2. Genomic Exploration and Conventional Scientific classification

In the domain of science, the combination of genomics with customary scientific categorization has changed how we might interpret biodiversity. DNA sequencing advances permit specialists to dig into the hereditary codes of organic entities, giving bits of knowledge into developmental connections and species separation. This approach supplements conventional scientific categorization, where morphological qualities are utilized for order. The collaboration among genomics and scientific categorization offers an all encompassing viewpoint on the variety of living things.

II. Protecting Social Legacy

1. **Computerized Chronicling and Preservation of Antiquities**
   In social protection, the joining of innovation with conventional strategies has introduced another period of advanced documenting and curio preservation. High-goal imaging, 3D filtering, and computer generated reality advancements empower the point by point documentation of verifiable antiques. This not just jelly sensitive things by decreasing actual taking care of yet in addition works with more extensive admittance to social legacy through virtual shows and instructive stages.

2. **Phonetics and Computerized Documentation of Dialects**

   The joint effort among innovation and customary etymology has become instrumental in reporting and saving jeopardized dialects. Advanced keep gadgets and record programming help etymologists in catching communicated in dialects, guaranteeing that etymological subtleties and social setting are saved. This combination adds to the documentation of etymological variety, which is significant for grasping mankind's set of experiences and social development.

   III. Natural Observing and Preservation

1. **Remote Detecting and Biological system Observation**
   In natural science, the joining of remote detecting advancements with customary field concentrates on improves our capacity to screen environments for an enormous scope. Satellite symbolism, robots, and sensor networks give constant information on ecological boundaries, permitting specialists to follow changes in biodiversity, deforestation, and environment designs. This far reaching approach supports the definition of powerful preservation systems and practical asset the board.

2. **Customary Natural Information and Current Preservation**

   The joining of conventional biological information (TEK) with current preservation rehearses makes a synergistic methodology that benefits both native networks and protection endeavors. Native people group, with their profound comprehension of neighborhood biological systems, contribute significant bits of knowledge that supplement logical information. Cooperative ventures, joining TEK and logical examination, cultivate local area commitment and upgrade the progress of protection drives.

   IV. Clinical Diagnostics and Medical care

1. **Telemedicine and Far off Understanding Observing**
   The coordination of innovation with conventional medical care rehearses has changed clinical diagnostics and patient consideration. Telemedicine stages and distant patient observing gadgets empower medical care experts

to arrive at patients in far off regions or screen persistent circumstances without the requirement for successive clinic visits. This approach further develops medical services availability, particularly in locales with restricted clinical foundation.

2. **Accuracy Medication and Genomic Diagnostics**

The union of genomics and conventional clinical diagnostics has brought about accuracy medication. Hereditary testing gives customized bits of knowledge into a singular's helplessness to specific sicknesses and their reaction to explicit therapies. This combination considers custom-made clinical mediations, streamlining treatment results and limiting antagonistic impacts.

V. Instructive Teaching method and Learning

1. **E-Learning Stages and Conventional Instructing Strategies**
   In schooling, the joining of innovation with customary showing strategies has reshaped the scene of learning. E-learning stages, intelligent reenactments, and virtual homerooms furnish understudies with admittance to an abundance of assets past conventional course readings. This mixed methodology improves understudy commitment, takes care of assorted learning styles, and gets ready people for the mechanically determined requests of the advanced labor force.

2. **Increased Reality (AR) and Involved Learning**

Expanded Reality (AR) applications upgrade involved opportunities for growth by overlaying computerized data onto the actual world. In fields, for example, life systems and designing, AR permits understudies to connect with virtual models, working with a more profound comprehension of complicated ideas. This combination of innovation and active learning overcomes any issues between hypothetical information and useful application.

VI. Difficulties and Contemplations

1. **Moral Contemplations and Security Concerns**
   The reconciliation of innovation and customary techniques accompanies moral contemplations, especially in regards to protection and information security. Specialists should explore the capable utilization of innovation, guaranteeing that information assortment and computerized chronicling regard people's privileges and social responsive qualities. Finding some kind of harmony between mechanical advancement and moral contemplations is urgent to keep up with public trust.

2. **Innovative Availability and Inclusivity**

While innovation offers gigantic advantages, guaranteeing its availability to assorted populaces is fundamental. Variations in mechanical access might prompt the prohibition of specific networks from the advantages of coordinated approaches. Specialists should take a stab at inclusivity, taking into account the innovative foundation and assets accessible to various gatherings.

VII. Future Bearings and Developments

1. **Progressions in Man-made reasoning (artificial intelligence) Mix**
   The eventual fate of coordinating innovation with customary strategies will probably observe huge progressions in computer based intelligence combination.
   AI calculations can examine tremendous datasets, perceive designs, and produce experiences that might evade conventional logical methodologies. This holds monstrous likely across different fields, from logical examination to medical services diagnostics and instructive investigation.

2. **Blockchain Innovation in Information Honesty**

   Blockchain innovation, known for its decentralized and secure nature, holds guarantee for guaranteeing information honesty in coordinated approaches. This development can improve straightforwardness and confidence in information sharing, particularly in cooperative exploration projects where various partners add to datasets. Blockchain's application in getting delicate data lines up with the developing accentuation on information morals.

   9.3 The potential impact of cranial research on broader scientific fields.
   Cranial exploration, with its unpredictable assessment of the skull's structure and capability, has the possibility to catalyze progressions across more extensive logical fields. The ramifications of cranial examinations stretch out past the domains of life systems and zoology, addressing assorted disciplines with extraordinary impacts.

   In fossil science, cranial exploration assumes a critical part in disentangling developmental chronicles. Fossilized skulls act as basic signs of species transformation and uniqueness. Through cranial investigation, scientistss reproduce old biological systems, follow the rise of new species, and perceive the ecological elements that molded transformative directions. The experiences acquired contribute fundamentally to how we might interpret Earth's natural past.

   In medication, the investigation of cranial life structures holds significant ramifications for diagnostics and treatment modalities. Neurological problems, awful wounds, and inherent circumstances frequently manifest in cranial designs. Headways in cranial examination upgrade the accuracy of clinical imaging, prompting more precise analyses and customized treatment plans. Furthermore, the investigation of cranial pathologies illuminates neurosurgeons and clinical professionals, directing restorative intercessions and surgeries.

The crossing point of cranial exploration with hereditary qualities opens roads in developmental hereditary qualities. By corresponding cranial highlights with hereditary varieties, specialists gain bits of knowledge into the atomic underpinnings of morphological variety. This interdisciplinary methodology improves our perception of how qualities impact skull advancement, giving a nuanced comprehension of transformative cycles.

Moreover, cranial exploration adds to more extensive biological examinations. Assessment of skull morphology in creature populaces helps with surveying natural specialties, hunter prey elements, and the effect of ecological changes on species endurance. This comprehensive point of view upholds protection endeavors by clarifying the complicated connections between cranial transformations and the environmental scene.

Fundamentally, cranial exploration fills in as a nexus, connecting different logical trains and cultivating a complete comprehension of life's complexities. Its effect resounds across fossil science, medication, hereditary qualities, and environment, enlightening different aspects of the regular world and propelling our aggregate information.